Understanding Emotions in Social Work

Understanding Emotions in Social Work

Theory, Practice and Reflection

Richard Ingram

 Open University Press

Open University Press
McGraw-Hill Education
McGraw-Hill House
Shoppenhangers Road
Maidenhead
Berkshire
England
SL6 2QL

email: enquiries@openup.co.uk
world wide web: www.openup.co.uk

and Two Penn Plaza, New York, NY 10121-2289, USA

First published 2015

A catalogue record of this book is available from the British Library

ISBN-13: 978-0-335-26386-8
ISBN-10: 0-335-26386-0
eISBN: 978-0-335-26387-5

Library of Congress Cataloging-in-Publication Data
CIP data applied for

Typeset by Transforma Pvt. Ltd., Chennai, India
Printed and bound by CPI Group (UK) Ltd, Croydon, CR0 4YY

Praise for this book

"This is a timely publication that reinforces the centrality of emotions and emotional intelligence in social work practice – a must read for all aspiring and practising social workers."

Gillian Ruch, Professor of Social Work, School of Education and Social Work,
University of Sussex, UK

"What Understanding Emotions in Social Work does is cuts across all layers of the social work curriculum and indeed the "resistance and lethargy" regarding "the role of emotions within social work practice" that Ingram refers to. It affords us with a medium through which to explore the substance of that which causes us to react and provides us with a space in which to learn more about what it means to respond; both to ourselves and to those we engage with.

It is a book for anyone involved in professional social work education and practice; one that will become a well-thumbed addition to the discerning practitioner's library."

Amanda M L Taylor, Senior Lecturer, School of Social Work,
University of Central Lancashire, UK

"Understanding Emotions in Social Work: Theory, practice and reflection, highlights the importance of emotion in social work practice. Dr Richard Ingram clearly makes the case that the recognition of, reflection upon, responsiveness to, and regulation of emotion, contributes to effective social work practice, as well as, the development of healthy practitioners and practice environments. This book reinforces how social work is primarily a human interactive and relational practice in which emotion and affect have a pivotal role. I highly recommend Understanding Emotions in Social Work as an essential text for students, social workers, supervisors and managers."

Associate Professor Kieran O'Donoghue, Head of School of Social Work,
Massey University, New Zealand

Dedication

For Aileen, Eve, Rosa, and Annie

Contents

Acknowledgements

I would like to take the opportunity to thank and acknowledge the contributions of people who have helped and supported me through the challenging process of turning my ideas into this book. I would like to thank the following people for their ideas and encouragement: Jane Fenton, Jennifer Harris, Alan Baird, Sharon Jackson, Timothy Kelly, Gillian Ruch, Roger Hennessey, Divya Jindal-Snape, and Patricia Fronek. I would also like to acknowledge the varied and illuminating contributions from colleagues, service users, and students over the course of my career, which underpin my interest in the emotional content of social work practice. The support from Katherine Hartle, Caroline Prodger, and Karen Harris from Open University Press/McGraw-Hill Education has been indispensable as I have progressed with the writing and structuring of the book.

Thanks must also go to Fiona Harrison for providing me with a bright and calm kitchen to think and write. Finally, I would like to thank my family for all their patience, love, encouragement, and humour from the start to finish of this endeavour.

Introduction

Why should we think about emotions and social work?

The concept of emotions is something that, as human beings, we know to be of importance within our relationships, experiences, and behaviours. We know this even without having to avail ourselves of the vast body of literature and research related to the topic. This is because it is something that is inescapably and intrinsically linked to the human experience and permeates all aspects of our lives. One would think that the centrality of emotions to our lives would be enough to place it at the core of social work practice, since the profession is concerned with individuals' lives and the complex factors that may affect their ability to function, thrive, and reach their potential. However, this book was inspired by the level of resistance and lethargy to the role of emotions within social work practice and how emotions impact on the relationships, decisions, and actions of social workers and service users.

If you were searching for this book online or picking your way through the bookshelves of a bookstore or library, you may have been struck by the paucity of literature making the link between emotions and social work within their title. Indeed, David Howe's (2008) *The Emotionally Intelligent Social Worker* is the only text to focus on the subject. This is of course not to say that emotions have been entirely neglected in social work literature, but they have tended to be linked to associated topics such as relationship-based practice (Ruch et al., 2010), skills (Hennessey, 2011), decision-making (O'Sullivan, 1999), professionalism (Brodie et al., 2008), and reflection (Ingram et al., 2014). Thus, it is hoped that this book will go some way to remedy this gap in the literature.

My interest in the subject of emotions in social work has its roots in a piece of research concerned with exploring the sources that students identified as contributing to their decision-making, as presented in their practice essays (Dowson et al., 2010). Unsurprisingly, students pointed to a range of sources, including theory, legislation, policy, supervision, and service user perspectives. What was particularly striking was that not one student in the cohort identified their emotions as contributing to their decision-making. This seemed at odds with my experiences as a social work practitioner and the discussions I had with students about their practice, in which the emotional content of practice was a key driver behind actions, motivation, and reflection. It was this absence that piqued my interest and led me to undertake a more focused exploration of the experiences and views of social workers in relation to emotions and practice (Ingram, 2013a). The fruits of this research will inform and underpin elements of this book, and help to shine a light on potential reasons for the lack of clarity around emotions in social work, including: professionalism; evidence-based practice; lack of opportunity; rational-technical working cultures and practices; and poor supervision.

It is encouraging that the focus of this book is also present explicitly and implicitly in a range of professional narratives and policies relating to the social work profession. For example, the Professional Capabilities Framework (PCF; College of Social Work, 2012) highlights that social workers need to engage in critical reflection, in which they examine facets of practice such as relationships, ethics, and use of self. The PCF makes explicit mention of the notion of emotional resilience and the need for social workers and social work students to be able to consider their well-being in relation to their practice. This clearly indicates the centrality of emotions in relation to the experience of being a social worker (let alone a human being). The British Association of Social Workers' Code of Ethics for Social Work (BASW, 2012b) echoes the need for social workers to engage in reflection and in so doing consider the relationships they form in practice and the ethical dimension therein (Ingram et al., 2014). The Munro Report (Munro, 2011) is explicit in its assertion that social workers need to be allowed greater autonomy and within that they should be permitted and supported to explore the complex emotional aspects of their practice. Indeed, Munro notes that the absence of the emotional experience of social work practice from social work discourse is of great concern in terms of allowing social workers to fully engage in the complexity of their practice. The Social Work Task Force report (DCSF, 2009) takes these themes further and highlights the need for high-quality supervision to facilitate the effective use of self and autonomy in relationships in practice. This is helpful because it recognizes the need for organizational and professional support for social workers to achieve effective autonomy.

In many ways, this is where this book comes in. The book will cover a range of key themes that will enable you to think about your own practice and the context in which it takes place. Readers of this book will adopt different ways of using and interpreting the material presented, which is a reflection of the uniqueness of each individual's emotional world. While there are many common cultural and professional cues to direct our emotional responses, these are interwoven with our own individual experiences and associated emotional worlds. The book will take you through a range of theoretical and practical topics and activities to support you as you engage in significant self-reflection and, in turn, enhanced self-knowledge. More generally, the book is intended to serve as a useful tool for students, practitioners, managers, and organizations to engage with the concept of emotions and how they do or do not impact on social work practice.

A guide to the learning features of this book

As noted above, this book cannot meaningfully be read in a detached theoretical manner. It should be read with one eye on your own experience (past and present) and you should reflect upon how your enhanced understanding of the concept of emotions and their place in social work practice affects your thinking about these experiences. The book is written in an accessible style to encourage the connections between your own experiences and the content of the book. To support you in this process, the book has been designed with a range of recurrent learning tools and features:

- *Learning objectives* – you will be provided with clear intended learning outcomes at the outset of each chapter. This will help you discern the relevance and focus of each chapter and help you tune into the key themes.
- *Case studies* – each chapter has a case study that reflects an engaging and relevant practice context to provide scaffolding and links between the chapter content and social work. The case studies are drawn from a range of social work contexts and are

designed to illustrate the complexities of the emotional aspects of practice, while promoting analysis and reflection. These are located early in chapters so that links and learning points can be made throughout.

- *Learning activities* – these will encourage you to consider the discussion from your own context and perspectives. This will make the book a useful resource for students and practitioners alike and help locate dilemmas, challenges, and opportunities that arise in practice within a clearer context. The activities can also be taken forward and used separate from the book in other forums such as supervision.
- *Voices of practitioners* – each chapter includes vivid and powerful quotes from social work practitioners across a range of practice settings. These are drawn from a research study that sought the views of a cohort of UK-based social work practitioners about the role of emotions within their practice (Ingram, 2013a). This feature is intended to underline the practical relevance of emotions across the range of practice contexts and highlight their complex and contested nature.
- *Key learning points* – these are presented in bullet point format at the end of each chapter to allow you to take stock of the content of each chapter and to identify future learning needs.
- *Further reading* – this will signpost you to relevant literature with a short synopsis indicating why it may be useful to your studies and/or practice.

A brief guide to the book

The book is split into two parts. The first is foundational in nature and presents the key conceptual underpinnings of emotions and locates these within the context of social work, while the second takes this more explicitly into the arena of practice and focuses on topics such as supervision, relationship-building, and organizational culture.

Part 1: What are emotions and why are they important in social work?

Chapter 1 provides a thorough exploration of the concept of emotions. It is evident that emotions as a concept are familiar yet slippery to grasp and articulate. The chapter draws from a range of sources, including neuroscience, cognitive psychology, psychoanalysis, sociology, and evolutionary theory. The chapter concludes with a conceptual framework based on a review of the literature. The framework recognizes that emotions have a biological underpinning and involve physiological sensations, cognitive appraisals, and have an impact on behaviour and expression. These elements are common across the literature and highlight the inescapable role that emotions have in the ways individuals make sense of their world, relate to others, and respond to events. This is placed within an individual and societal context whereby cultures, norms, rules, and experiences contribute to the ways emotions are appraised and expressed. This framework provides you with an inclusive 'definition' of emotions that will inform you as your proceed through the book.

Chapter 2 takes the framework proposed in Chapter 1 and establishes links with social work practice. In many ways, this chapter provides a rationale for the book by identifying the areas in which you are most likely to find emotions salient and/or contested. Key themes are introduced and contextualized, including relationship-based practice, care ethics, professionalism, rational-technical approaches, decision-making, reflection, and self-awareness. These themes are interwoven throughout the book and will give you a sense of the terrain.

Chapter 3 underlines that reflection is a crucial and necessary process for social workers to engage in if emotions are to be acknowledged, managed, and used in social work practice. A range of approaches to reflection will be proposed with the intention of providing you with a toolkit for engaging in the rest of the book but also taking the learning forward into your practice. Reflection is broadened out to encompass a range of pertinent factors such as the inter-personal, intra-personal, cultural, organizational, and professional strands of practice. Links will also be made to emotional intelligence. This provides us with a concept that involves the explicit identification, appraisal, management, and use of emotions within ourselves and others.

Part 2: Applying and understanding emotions in social work practice

Chapter 4 establishes the links with relationship-based approaches to practice. It is recognized that social work relationships are complex and are infused with emotional content and communication. Such relationships require inter- and intra-personal awareness and skills to manage these complexities, and messages from the service user-led literature underpin the centrality of qualities such as warmth, empathy, and emotional attunement. Empathy in particular will be highlighted as a key concept and one that is inextricably linked with emotional intelligence and the social work relationship. Links will be made with social work practice skills and the role that emotions have in guiding, motivating, and compromising these skills will be discussed and examined.

Chapter 5 focuses on the role of emotions within the various forms of writing in social work. The importance of writing in terms of communication and recording is explored, and the uncomfortable place that emotions have within this sphere is highlighted. This leads the discussion to consider issues such as professionalism and how this may be perceived as a barrier to writing about the emotional content of practice. The removal or editing of emotions from the written articulation of practice raises questions about transparency and accuracy, and these will be explored.

Chapter 6 focuses on the sources of support and opportunities for reflection that social workers can access and utilize in practice. A range of approaches to supervision will be considered and the impact that this may have on the exploration of emotions will be highlighted. Social workers, of course, access support and guidance from many sources, including informal peer support, group supervision, and self-reflection. The chapter suggests how you may navigate your way through the maze of support and supervision to facilitate consideration of the emotional content of your practice.

Chapter 7 looks at the place of emotions within organizational culture. The chapter examines familiar concepts such as managerialism and bureaucracy through a lens that seeks to consider how the emotional content of practice is nurtured or marginalized. The chapter is intended to provide you with the means to assess your own organizational context and consider how it impacts your practice and your emotions therein. Messages from a range of social work narratives are highlighted, and the increasing emphasis on learning cultures and learning practitioners is identified as a useful vehicle for emotions to become embedded in practice.

Chapter 8 pulls the key strands of the book together, culminating in a model that firmly embeds emotions within social work practice and discourse. The proposed model will forge explicit links between professional frameworks, practice, organizational culture, and practitioner supports to create a vision of the profession that facilitates and accommodates the emotional aspects of practice. A key aspect of this model will be the removal of perceived barriers between these elements, which previously created a climate where the emotional aspects of practice could be seen as being in competition or incongruous with the technical-rational aspects of social work. The concepts of professionalism and professional identity will also be examined to help you locate your own place within the model and to support you to identify the strengths and weaknesses of your current context.

Due to the interplay between the theoretical-practical content of the book and your own unique and ever-changing practice experiences, it is hoped that this book will provide a useful introduction to the topic of emotions but also a resource to be returned to repeatedly as you encounter new challenges and opportunities within your practice.

Part 1
What are emotions and why are they important in social work?

Part 1 of this book provides readers with the conceptual, practical, and critical underpinnings of the subject matter and will allow them to engage fully with the contextualized aspects of Part 2. The book begins with an overview of the concept of emotions, drawn from a range of perspectives, including neuroscience, social psychology, and behavioural psychology. These strands and perspectives are then pulled together to create a conceptual framework. This also allows readers to proceed with clarity and confidence about the concept of emotions and its centrality to human behaviour and experience.

Light is then shed on the presence and use of emotions in social work practice. The key themes of relationship-based practice, care ethics, professionalism, rational-technical approaches, decision-making, reflection, and self-awareness are introduced, and readers are encouraged to consider their own experiences and contexts. This is further reinforced by the focus on reflection in Chapter 3, which underlines that our understanding and use of emotions require significant thought and analysis. A variety of reflective approaches are considered to help support active engagement in critical reflection, and in turn the role that emotions should have within this.

1 | What are emotions?

Chapter objectives

This chapter will:

- Examine the concept of emotions from a range of research perspectives.
- Make links between these differing perspectives and develop a conceptual framework that will provide the foundations for the rest of this book.
- Link the framework of emotions to the case study example and wider social work issues.
- Encourage you to consider your own experiences and views on emotions in the light of the framework proposed.

Emotions: setting the scene

The topic of emotions is an interesting one to approach as a student or practitioner since it is very likely that you will come to this book with a sense of what emotions are and what they mean to you. It is very difficult to navigate your way through any given day without being required to report how you are feeling about a range of situations and relationships. It is equally likely that you will make a range of decisions and judgements based on your emotional responses that will direct your behaviour and contribute to the person you are, both internally and externally. Despite the ubiquitous role of emotions in everyday life, you will also view emotions through a range of cultural lenses, which will impact on: which stimuli will trigger emotional responses; what the nature of those responses will be; how you will express and communicate those responses; and how others around you may react. For example, as a reader involved in social work, you may approach this book with some uncertainty as to the role that emotion *should* play in practice, and whether emotions are likely to cloud professional judgement. Indeed, you may be considering for the first time what the familiar term 'emotion' means to you. The issues noted in this paragraph touch on some of the issues explored in this chapter and begin the journey towards a clearer understanding of the concept of emotions, which will then inform and underpin the remainder of the book.

When seeking a conceptual framework with which to understand and examine emotions, one is confronted with a plethora of perspectives and approaches that can seem to make the concept rather diffuse if taken in isolation. This chapter seeks to review the key tenets of the literature relating to emotions and in doing so establish a coherent and accommodating framework that will help us locate emotions more clearly within the context of social work. Indeed, it will be seen that the boundaries between perspectives have been lowered in recent years and that emotion is increasingly being understood as a concept that requires a broad definition rather than one simply tied to one school of thought. There is still no widely accepted concept of emotions, and Barrett (2012) notes that despite the volume of research across disciplines, it is difficult to unite the 'hard' streams of data (i.e. neurological imaging) with the 'soft' streams of data (i.e. the subjective explanations of individuals) to create a cohesive whole.

This chapter will begin by looking at emotions from an evolutionary perspective (Darwin, 1890) and notes the early inclusion of physiology, cognition, and purpose within the construct of emotions. These facets will be explored further and a clearer sense of definitions and the landscape of emotions research will be provided. The chapter will then explore the contributions of neuroscience to our understanding of the role of brain function and underline the importance of the appraisal of emotions. The appraisal of the *meaning* that emotional responses have is crucial when considering their role in social work, and this opens the door to considering how these meanings are individually and culturally nuanced and generated. Emotions will be seen to be functional and purposeful, which will helpfully link with relationship-building and motivations to engage with others. The expression and presentation of emotions are a key element, and are further influenced by context, culture, and experience. The chapter concludes with a conceptual framework of emotions, which will serve as your working understanding of the concept as you move around the remainder of the book.

Case study

Sofia is a newly qualified social work practitioner and is coming to the end of her first month working within a hospital social work team. The team works across all service user groups in a large general hospital, and offers support to patients while in the hospital and takes a lead role in planning and securing packages of care upon discharge.

Sofia has found the challenge of settling into a new role while managing an expanding workload very demanding. The team seems very welcoming and friendly, although Sofia is struggling to remember the names and roles of individual team members and has found it hard to find time to sit down and chat with colleagues over lunch.

Sofia began working with an 18-year-old woman called Rachel on her first day in post. Rachel was being looked after in an oncology ward and had been diagnosed with terminal cancer. Sofia's key role was to provide therapeutic support to Rachel and to plan for Rachel's request to return home for the final stages of her illness. Sadly, Rachel died in hospital 3 weeks after Sofia became involved. Sofia feels privileged to have established a positive relationship with Rachel at such a difficult stage in her illness, but also has found herself feeling tearful and guilty that she could not have facilitated the desired move home. In the meantime, Sofia's caseload continues to grow and her supervisor (whom she has met three times) is very positive about her progress so far.

- What might Sofia be feeling as she enters her first qualified social work position? Think about the plethora of variables involved: clarity of role, team culture, lack of experience, ambitions and status, establishing relationships, understanding processes and procedures, and so on.

- The death of Rachel is clearly of significance to Sofia – how might she react emotionally? How do you feel Sofia *should* react as a social worker?
- Try to think of yourself in similar circumstances (you may have had experiences that chime closely with the above example) and how you might feel. Why do you think you will feel that way?

Emotions: evolution towards cognition

Charles Darwin (1890) contributed significantly to our understanding of emotions from an evolutionary perspective. His contention was that emotions have their roots in early animal life and have evolved as a means of alerting us to dangers and situations that require us to react and respond. Jenkins et al. (1998) note that this introduces us to the potential *functionality* of emotions. By this they mean that emotional responses and their associated behaviours can fulfil a crucial role in terms of serving our needs and goals. For example, they note that the familiar paradigm of 'freezing with fear' may be understood within the context of making oneself less visible to danger, yet this physiological reaction then becomes viewed as a universal expression of fear. Writing in the context of social work, Howe (2008) notes that Darwin's focus on the physiological sensations of emotions are crucial for providing individuals with fast links to sets of behaviours that will help us to respond appropriately and also to guide us to focus on what is important.

Darwin (1890) introduced the notion of emotional expression (to be returned to repeatedly in this chapter) as a key component. He suggested that some emotional responses appear to be involuntary physiological reactions to stimuli that are linked to hereditary reactions to danger. For example, one may experience fear while watching a horror film, despite knowing that it is a fictional portrayal of events. Darwin noted that young infants exhibit fear responses to stimuli such as loud rattles at an age and stage when this cannot be rooted in direct experience. This is a key facet of the claims for certain emotional responses being inherited through evolution. He stated that there is a habitual element to emotional expression that develops over time, which may in fact (as with the horror film example) not even have a clear purpose.

Turner and Stets (2005) highlight the influential legacy of Darwin's research on the consistency of facial expression across cultures. In exploring emotional expression across cultures, Ekman (1977, 1989) was able to identify commonalities that exist regardless of cultural norms and context. So, for example, the expression of joy and happiness through the use of a smile was found to resonate and communicate across global and cultural boundaries. This link to Darwin is crucial and represents a key foundation stone for considering emotions to be at one level a universal phenomenon. This approach to considering emotions across cultures moves our thinking about emotions into an area of context, norms, and culture that will be examined in more detail later in the chapter. Furthermore, Jenkins et al. (1998) note that Darwin's notion that there are universal elements relating to the biological and genetic sources of emotions opened the door to the neurological work undertaken in the latter stages of the twentieth century (see Damasio, 2000).

The psychologist William James (1890), writing about emotions at the same time as Darwin, emphasized that emotions cannot be detached from the physiological sensation they are linked to. James described these as '*sensational processes*' (p. 28), which add the depth to what otherwise would merely be one-dimensional perceptions. He also noted that although emotions are usually associated with an 'object', that object need not necessarily be present but can be simply thought about or remembered. This allows us to consider emotions in terms of conscious and unconscious spheres. The influential James-Lange theory of emotions suggests that an event or stimulus provokes a physiological reaction, and our interpretation of this reaction identifies the emotion involved. If we consider the case study, it may be that Sofia has a sense of anxiety (for example, 'butterflies in her stomach') when starting her new post, the source of which she may not be able to identify but which will impact on her experience of her new role. This physiological feeling is only really useful to Sofia if she continues to examine and appraise it to uncover its source and its *meaning* to her.

Schachter and Singer (1962) developed the two-factor theory of emotion that was inspired by the emerging notion of appraisal. Their contention was that an emotion is created by a physiological sensation followed by a labelling of it that is drawn from available information and cues. Briefly, this research involved participants being injected with medication that raised their blood pressure and then being given differing explanations for what they would feel. For example, participants were told they would feel excited or, alternatively, fearful. These suggestions provided persuasive cues for the labelling of the emotion. Maslach (1979) built on the research of Schachter and Singer (1962) and found that this was not always reproducible and that suggested cues often simply led to confusion and anxiety. We will see, however, that the notion of appraisal and labelling of emotions is still very evident in emotional discourse today (Barrett, 2012). This helps us to understand Sofia's situation further, in that she will draw from her previous experiences (personal and professional) and from the cultural cues of her agency to inform how she should respond to feelings of loss. Her ability to manage this may well be reliant on the quality and congruency of the information she is able to draw upon. For example, in a hospital setting, the process of new patients filling beds of recently deceased patients can give a powerful message to workers about the pace of 'moving on', which may be at odds with Sofia's personal experiences and norms regarding responses to death.

The above discussion touches on concepts that require definition. Turner and Stets (2005) note that emotions, feelings, and moods are often used interchangeably within the literature relating to emotions. Jenkins et al. (1998) recognize that these are all part of what we might call the broad landscape of emotional discourse. Damasio (2000) suggests that feelings are private and internal rather than expressed. Turner and Stets (2005) note that for something to constitute a feeling, it must by definition be *consciously* felt. Howe (2008) suggests that feelings also apply purely to the physiological aspect of emotional arousal, and that it becomes an emotion once it is cognitively appraised and labelled. For the purposes of this book, 'feelings' will be used to refer to consciously felt emotions only, although these may well be unclear and ambiguous to the individual experiencing them. The term 'emotions' will be used to include unconscious aspects of emotions and be useable across the various paradigms discussed in this chapter. The notion of 'moods' will be referred to less frequently, but can be understood to represent longer-term emotional states and dispositions that may be less affected by changing events or stimuli, but nevertheless are part of what the literature and you may view as part of your emotional world. Moods, it is argued, impact on the aforementioned *appraisal* of events and affect which aspects of a situation one is likely to focus on (Davidson, 1994).

The preceding discussion introduces the key foundations for the multi-faceted conceptualization of emotions and the associated schools of thought that emerged during the twentieth century. We will now explore the key aspects of these perspectives in greater detail.

Emotions: a neurological perspective

The world of neuroscience might seem a rather daunting place to look for clarity on the processes of emotions, but it actually provides us with a relatively concrete source of information about the importance of brain functioning and emotion. This is helpful because prior to developments such as brain imaging, emotions research was dominated by observations, interpretations, and individual subjective accounts (Howe, 2008). It is important to remember that while the brain has emerged as a core *processor* of emotions, humans still require exposure to experiences and situations to feed information into the neurological systems for emotional responses and judgements to be made. This underlines the individuality and ever-evolving nature of emotions and emotional appraisal. In the preface to their edited book on the cognitive neuroscience of emotions, Lane and Nadel (2000) noted that developments in brain imaging, and the consequent blossoming of the evidence base for understanding the workings of the human brain, have raised the concept of emotions to an observable and in turn concrete concept that ranks alongside other mental processes such as memory and attention in terms of conceptual clarity.

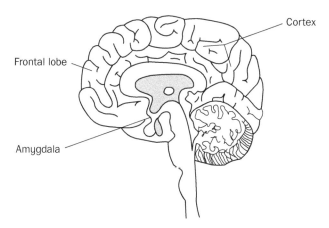

Figure 1.1 The location of the amygdala, frontal lobe, and cortex
Source: Adapted from Glassman and Hadad (2013)

Damasio (1994) and LeDoux (1993) undertook research examining the decision-making of individuals with damage to their amygdala (see Figure 1.1), which provides a useful indication of the pivotal role of this part of the brain in terms of emotions. LeDoux (1993) proposed that the amygdala is the central emotional hub of the brain, based on the observation that individuals who experience damage to this part of the brain display significantly impaired emotional responses. Damasio (1994) suggested that damage to the amygdala led individuals to lose prior emotional learning (i.e. impact of behaviour on others) and thus to make decisions in their lives that led to negatives outcomes (i.e. relationship breakdown). However, it was noted that there was no impact on IQ scores as a result of this impairment. This contributes to the view that the amygdala has a specific neural function relating to the processing of emotions and contributes to the concrete evidence base that emotions have a clear neurological basis. This research also noted the role of emotional learning, which allows for links to be made to social context and the impact of prior experiences and cultural scripts. LeDoux (1997) considered these findings in the context of the familiar conditioning research of Pavlov. LeDoux noted that when individuals are conditioned through repeated exposure to negative stimuli to avoid a particular object, the emotion of fear is eventually expunged, leaving simple avoidance behaviour by association. However, as time goes by, the conditioned response may diminish and brief re-exposure to the negative stimuli is required. It is at this point that the amygdala draws upon previous emotional experience to guide the response.

LeDoux (1997) identified the amygdala and neo-cortex as key. The amygdala is the area of the brain that allows us to make quick emotional responses, whereas the neo-cortex is the area that applies reason and evaluation to initial emotional responses. These processes happen in conjunction with each other and from a neurological perspective present an initial two-step process of physiological response followed by cognitive appraisal. For example, on hearing a loud bang, your amygdala allows for an immediate response in terms of your safety (move away quickly), while the neo-cortex helps you then consider where the bang came from and in turn appraise the degree of risk involved. This is a useful example to illustrate the interplay between the cognitive and neurological parts of emotional processing. Pennebaker (1980) further underlined this physiological and cognitive process in experiments involving the administration of chemicals to induce the physiological symptoms of fear. He found that participants did not report feelings of fear despite the physiological sensation of it. This underlines the role of appraisal and judgement.

Damasio et al. (1991) undertook research into the impact of damage to the frontal lobe on emotions. They found that there was a loss of somatic markers (previously developed associations between physiological reactions and emotions) that help us to think about complex situations. They drew links with the notion of 'gut feeling', which draws on previous knowledge and experiences to help us identify and trigger emotional responses and reasoning. We will return to the notion of 'gut feeling' and its close relative 'professional wisdom' throughout this book. What is important at this stage is to note that previous experience will help shape our reactions to events (and will have contributed to Sofia's reactions in the case study) and allow opportunities for reflection rather than suppression or denial.

Writing from a sociological viewpoint, Turner and Stets (2005) argue that neurological processes trigger emotional responses that are then understood, expressed, and constrained by the social contexts within which they are experienced. Despite their sociological emphasis, they concede that emotions cannot be viewed purely as a socially constructed entity, as they acknowledge that the physiological aspect of emotions can in some circumstances be so profound that they override social scripts and norms (i.e. when the intensity of anger erupts publicly). In relation to the significant feelings of grief experienced by Sofia in the case study, one can see the interaction between the physiological reaction (tears) and the social context (the role of a social worker within a hospital setting).

There may be times when we respond to emotional memories and may need to be told externally about our behaviours (i.e. being defensive within an interaction). Turner and Stets (2005) concede that unconscious emotions rather than conscious ones are problematic from a sociological standpoint, as they appear by definition to occur outside of the culturally nuanced conscious sphere. For example, Sofia may subconsciously avoid exploring her grief reaction due to unconscious memories. These remain an internal process unless they are brought to light through reflection or the prompting of others (Rosenberg, 1990). Turner and Stets (2005) note that the binary debate between biological and cultural perspectives is unhelpful, as both aspects are key components of emotions. Put simply, they argue that the initial physiological response is then understood within the context of cultural scripts, goals, and meanings and that neither can exist without the other. Barrett (2012) concurs with this view and criticizes the continuing tendency to seek divisions within research.

Emotions: cognition and appraisal

> . . . we do not simply 'feel' an emotion; we also 'think' an emotion.
>
> (Rosenberg, 1990: 5)

Since the work of James (1890), the role of cognition has secured a place within the conceptual framework of emotions. The role of thought, and the timing and ways in which it is involved in emotional processing and expression, vary. What seems to be constant is the role that thought and appraisal have in lending meaning to physiological and neurological arousal. LeDoux (1997) noted the intertwined relationship between the rapid response of the amygdala and the secondary reasoning of the cortex areas of the brain. He noted that these processes bring together the physiological and the cognitive. Turner and Stets (2005) suggested that cognitive approaches to conceptualizing emotions are concerned with the appraisal and judgements we apply to felt emotions. Rosenberg (1990) noted that this potentially moves emotional processing into a reflexive arena, whereby we add depth and detail to the physiological aspects of emotion by thinking about the relationship between our emotions, sensations, and thoughts. It is through this process that we develop a keener sense of our 'self' and in turn can begin to manage and regulate our emotions accordingly. We will focus on the role of reflection later in the book, but note here that having the opportunity to think about our responses is essential if we are to make sense of our practice. In the context of the case study, Sofia would benefit from being given an opportunity in supervision to take a step back from her practice and all the significant events that have occurred in her first few weeks in the job. This would allow her to unpick the personal meanings that she has applied to those events and the factors that underpin these meanings.

Lane et al. (2000) note that although cognitive appraisals are usually conscious, they are not necessarily so. They recognize that conceptually this presents a challenge to the cognitive neuroscience perspective, as the boundaries between the unconscious and conscious are not clear or easily definable. They argue that the definition of cognition should embrace both aspects of consciousness and that these are linked to wider neural processes such as memory and perception.

Lazarus and Lazarus (1994: 151) state that 'an emotion is a personal life drama, which has to do with the fate of our goals in a particular encounter and our beliefs about ourselves and the world we live in. It is aroused by an appraisal of the personal significance or meaning of what is happening in that encounter.' This fundamental centrality to human experience suggests that emotions are crucial in helping us consider courses of actions (Davidson, 1994; Lazarus and Lazarus, 1994; Turner and Stets, 2005). Emotions are aroused when a person perceives that something they desire comes to fruition or is compromised. Goleman (1995) echoes this goal-orientated view of emotions, and makes explicit links between goal attainment and emotional awareness and regulation. Alongside the emphasis on goals, it is important that we remember the emotional responses contained within the process towards goals and also the interplay between competing goals that we may hold. For example, Sofia's response to the death of Rachel is in part regret at not being able to fulfil her final wish to return home, but also is to do with the relationship that developed between them. There are also other mediating variables at play such as the unpredictability of Rachel's illness and the constraints of resources and processes that Sofia must abide by in her practice.

Jenkins et al. (1998) concur with this goal-orientated view of emotions and state that if we are aware of an emotion, then by definition we are aware that it is related to something that is of importance to us, whether that be negative or positive. This process of appraisal requires us to attach a label to our emotions and in turn this opens up a range of options in terms of our subsequent actions. Fridja (1988) approaches emotions from a cognitive psychology perspective and suggests that emotions must have a *situational meaning*. This adds a layer of complexity to the notion of appraisal, since we cannot simply identify an event/object and conclude that a particular emotion will be evoked; rather, we need to explore the meaning that it has in relation to wider goals and events. For example, in providing support to a relative of Rachel immediately after her death, Sofia will need to try to understand the meaning that this event has for them. It may be that Rachel played a significant part in this person's life and that a number of secondary losses (Currer, 2007) add to the depth of the emotional response of grief. Alternatively, it may be that they had a very distant relationship and the impact on the relative is not so great. Even this example makes some casual assumptions about context and likely emotional impact, and as such underlines the need for a flexible and individualized approach to considering emotions and appraisal of meaning. In terms of social work practice, this sits comfortably with the ethos of seeking the views of service users and relationship-based approaches to practice (Hennessey, 2011).

Searle (2010) notes that the meanings that we apply to events, and in turn our emotional responses to them are subjectively constructed individually and culturally. Barrett (2012) offers an interesting example of our reactions to weeds and flowers. She notes that the low status we afford a weed changes its social meaning and in turn drives our feelings and behaviour towards it. Figure 1.2 shows a picture of a rose and a dandelion. Putting the social meaning of these to one side momentarily, it is possible to elicit a

Figure 1.2 The social meaning of flowers and weeds

similar emotional response to each in terms of their attractiveness as examples of plant life. As soon as we consider the classification of flowers and weeds, then our emotional responses change. This introduces the impact of social construction and consensus, which contribute to our appraisals of events and stimuli. This same process can be applied within a social work context in the sense that our thresholds regarding the risk of substance misuse and parenting are driven in part by the labels we attach to both activities and their perceived degree of compatibility.

Fridja (1988) concurs with Lazarus (1991) that appraisal is an ongoing process. Fridja suggests that individuals undertake primary and secondary appraisals, which produce an evolving and subjective management of emotions. For example, Sofia may have discussed in depth Rachel's fears of dying in hospital and will have supported her during her initial emotional reaction of fear, but will also have had an eye to supporting Rachel to consider (secondary appraisal) the possible medical benefits of remaining in hospital. This example reflects the complex multi-faceted range of emotions and emotional appraisals that may be undertaken in any given situation.

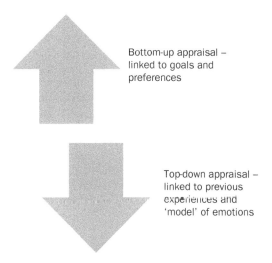

Bottom-up appraisal – linked to goals and preferences

Top-down appraisal – linked to previous experiences and 'model' of emotions

Figure 1.3 Bottom-up versus top-down appraisal

Source: Based on Clore and Ortony (2000)

Clore and Ortony (2000) note that appraisal may happen at a conscious or unconscious level. A 'bottom-up' approach to appraisal is a conscious process whereby our emotions reflect our goals, preferences, and experiences. Alternatively, a 'top-down' approach involves emotions being triggered by previous experience and indeed previous appraisal (Figure 1.3). For example, a key aspect of attachment theory is the notion that prior learning can unconsciously shape our emotional reactions to events later in life through the development of emotional models. This clearly links to the need to seek opportunities to reflect upon and explore the sources of our reactions and associated actions. Rosenberg (1990) talks of the importance of prior social learning when appraising events on an emotional level. He suggests that this gives individuals an *emotional logic*, achieved through linking previous experiences to a presenting event/object.

Voices of practitioners: Simone, a children and families social worker

'A feeling of anxiety is my way of knowing that there is something that is not quite right about a situation . . . this has naturally led me to be more curious, perhaps ask more questions, etc. Generally, there are further concerns that are only uncovered by asking the right questions.'

It is clear that Simone is highlighting a physiological feeling that she is able to label 'anxiety'. This is not something she can immediately locate the source of, but instead will be based on knowledge gained through previous experience and events. It is very important and heartening that this appraisal is then linked to further analysis and action, and provides a source of motivation and direction for her practice.

Emotions: social construction, culture, and expression

Turner and Stets (2005) state that a sociological perspective of emotions views them as being socially constructed in the sense that they are responses to prevailing cultural norms. They accept that this social construction operates in conjunction with the biological aspects of emotions but that the meaning that emotions attain and their importance within society are by definition a social entity. They place particular emphasis on the role of culture (in the context of this book, organizational and professional culture emerge as key themes) and how this impacts on the meanings we apply to events, and in turn the manner in which we express the ensuing emotions. They sum up their view as follows:

> Emotions are the driving force behind the commitments to culture. Indeed emotions are what give cultural symbols the very meanings and power to regulate, direct, and channel human behaviour and to integrate patterns of social organisation.
>
> (Turner and Stets, 2005: 292)

The notion that cultural context is crucial may appear to challenge the sense that there is a universality to emotions. Jankowiak and Fischer (1992) undertook a cross-cultural study of folkloric materials to examine the universality of the emotion of love. Their findings strongly pointed towards its universality, but noted that the opportunity to experience the emotion and the ways in which the emotion was expressed were impacted by culture. This is useful when considering the social work context, as the emotions engendered by practice such as happiness and fear may be common across all contexts, but may be subject to variance in organizational cultures in terms of how these are expressed and/or recorded. In relation to Sofia, it is likely that she will need to strike a balance between the felt emotion of loss and the expectations of professional presentation, which may compromise the appropriateness of crying. This begins to form links between professionalism and emotions, which will be discussed later. A further example of cross-cultural research is that of Ekman and Friesen (1971), who explored the universality of facial expressions and associated emotions between New Guinea and western cultures. They found a strong sense that there were universal, emotionally driven facial expressions (i.e. smiling and happiness), but the event/object that elicited such emotions varied across cultures. In relation to social work, this again suggests that the professional context may have an impact upon which emotions social workers feel and how they are expressed.

Barrett (2012) also usefully points out that there is no 'one-size-fits-all' relationship between emotions and behaviours. So, for example, the emotion of fear may be linked to defensiveness, flight or freezing. This further muddies the waters when making comparisons across cultures or indeed between individuals.

There are useful links to be made here with the work of Hochschild. In her seminal book *The Managed Heart* (1983), Hochschild considered the 'act' of presenting yourself in line with the requirements and culture of the context in which you are employed. She drew vividly on the experiences of flight attendants and the strong organizational culture of customer service and the associated emphasis on smiling. Hochschild noted that flight attendants are required to smile regardless of their true feelings and emotional reactions to their work or the people with whom they interact. She termed the underlying process of emotional management and presentation *emotional labour*. This labour intensifies when there is a tension between required behaviours and felt emotions. For example, if we consider the balance between the technical/rational and relationship-based aspects of social work as a feature of the cultural context in which social workers operate, then we can begin to consider Hochschild's concept of 'acting' in relation to the need to consider one's professional presentation. Mann (2004) suggests that emotional labour is either faking one's emotions, hiding one's emotions or managing one's emotions to fit with one's context.

Hochschild (1983) noted two distinct types of acting within any given cultural context:

- *Surface acting*: when one tries to deceive another by making them think we are feeling something we are not.
- *Deep acting*: when one tries to train oneself to act in a particular way that is underpinned by a set of rules or norms.

At the heart of Hochschild's work is a focus on how professionals control the expression of their emotions in their attempts to conform to *cultural* or *emotion ideologies* around emotional responses. She argues that the acquisition of these emotion ideologies is achieved through socialization processes. It is clear that for Sofia, at such an early stage in her practice experience, these cultural expectations may be vague and uncertain.

Learning activity

- Can you identify the prevailing culture within an agency in which you have practised?
- What impact does this have on the way you express emotions?
- What are the positives and negatives of adjusting emotional expression to fit with organizational cultures?

Hochschild makes a bold assumption that your emotions can be readily interchanged with the requirements of the organization in which you work. As you are reading this, you may or may not recognize this as true to your practice. Bolton and Boyd (2003) repeated Hochschild's research of flight cabin crews to explore whether workers were able and/or willing to trade their own individual emotional responses for those desired by the organization for which they worked. They were driven by an interest in the apparent marginalization of private/individual emotions (prior to Hochschild's work the most common paradigm of emotions) in the face of an overpowering social context.

They were interested in whether the smile of the flight attendants was their *own* smile or the *company's* smile. The researchers found that the flight attendants were emotionally dexterous and were able to locate themselves within the organizational context rather than fully give themselves over to it. Bolton and Boyd noted that participants talked of secondary socialization into the norms and codes of the organization but also found space for their long-held personal beliefs, experiences, and norms from their primary socialization. This resonates with the idea of *emotional displays* suggested by Rosenberg (1990), whereby the emotions we display can be distinctly purposeful and strategic. This is potentially very interesting for social work, as it notes the place that cultural guidance (e.g. codes of practice) may have in terms of impacting on emotional responses and the impact of personal values and experiences. This mirrors the familiar debates in social work about the balance between personal and professional values (Dominelli, 2009). A further finding from Bolton and Boyd's (2003) research that is pertinent to this discussion is that participants stated their actions were often driven by internal emotional responses that made them 'go the extra mile' regardless of organizational rules or norms. Anecdotally, when I ask new students why they have chosen social work as a profession, they often refer to 'wanting to make a difference' or 'a commitment to helping people and social justice'. While the realities of practice and organizational culture may constrain or clash with this at times, perhaps there is an indication here that social workers may still find space for their own personal and individual emotional worlds.

Zapf (2002) noted that the organizational cultural requirement of some professions is that emotional expression should be genuine. This clearly has links to social work, since genuineness is widely considered a desirable characteristic of social workers (Lishman, 2009). Bolton (2000) asked nurses to recount their experiences of emotional expression within their role. Interestingly, respondents reported that where positive reassurance was being offered to individuals whose prognosis was poor or who presented challenging behaviour, they were able to override the apparent dissonance between emotion and action by drawing on their own motivations to become nurses. Simply put, they were able to locate a congruency between the expression of calmness and their professional role, despite perhaps internally experiencing different emotions. This suggests that contextual issues can be multi-layered, and that any dissonance can be ameliorated through drawing on wider socio-professional constructs. This clearly has potential resonance within the social work context.

Rosenberg (1990) suggests that there may be a further aspect to the influence of cultural and contextual expectations upon our expression and our actions, namely *social consensus*. Given the above discussion on the potential impact of organizational culture, it suggests that we need to take cognizance of the influence of observation and role-modelling within teams and organizations and the potential this has for encouraging individuals to express their emotions in line with those of others around them (consider the aforementioned example of the rapid replacement of patients in hospital beds following their death). Within a social work context, this can set the tone for how and where emotions are expressed, but may also present an opportunity for organizational culture to purposefully and powerfully create an environment that reduces the potential for the professional dissonance considered within the work of Hochschild.

Emotions: psychoanalytic perspectives

This chapter has noted that emotional arousal is often associated with identifiable stimuli or objects. In these circumstances, it is possible for individuals to be able to articulate the source of their response, the physiological impact this has, and the meaning they are able to apply to it. Trevithick (2003) would argue that the 'known' elements of emotional experience are only part of the picture. Trevithick suggests psychoanalytic perspectives have much to offer in relation to highlighting and unpicking the less visible and often unconscious emotional worlds of individuals.

Psychoanalytic theories have their roots in the work of Freud (see, for example, Freud, 1959) and in particular the emphasis on understanding and recognizing the impact of previous experiences (often repressed or unconscious) on current responses and behaviours. Ruch (2009) acknowledges a debt to the work of Freud in the context of social work practice and reflection. The notion that individuals possess unconscious emotional markers and experiences is congruent with the idea that emotions are inescapably part of the private world of an individual (Barrett, 2012). Ruch (2009) notes that unconscious emotional drivers are a crucial source of information for social workers, which help them to understand the dynamics of relationships and their responses to different events.

John and Trevithick (2012) suggest that in the context of social work, supervision has a role to play in allowing social workers to explore and uncover the emotions at play in their relationships with service users. The work of Bion (1962) is hugely influential in this area. Bion highlighted the notion of 'containment' as being crucial in helping individuals gain emotional insight. Simply put, this refers to the conditions that allow for the integration of thinking and feeling. For example, John and Trevithick (2012) suggest that encouragement and reframing are two possible aspects of a containing relationship. In a sense, Bion (1962) was expanding the dynamics of a psychotherapeutic relationship to other contexts. Bion was particularly interested in the anxieties felt by individuals involved in group processes. He highlighted the role of group facilitator as crucial in terms of identifying anxieties within a group but also, and most crucially, explicitly naming them and highlighting them to the group members. Ruch (2009) argues that putting the unconscious emotional sphere under the spotlight is essential to avoid the negative effects of emotional suppression. For example, Hair (2012) found that social workers who lacked opportunities to explore their feelings in supervision experienced higher levels of stress. One can see the links with a containing supervisory relationship and the cognitive aspects of emotional appraisal and understanding discussed earlier. Ruch (2009) notes that the ability to gain insight into the unconscious and less rational aspects of behaviour is not only crucial to understanding one's own emotional responses, but also the ability to understand the emotional world of the people with whom we work.

Another key feature of the psychoanalytic perspective is an emphasis on the interpersonal aspects of emotions. In the previous section, we noted that emotions can be purposeful and can be influential and communicated within interactions. Agass (2002) highlights the important concepts of transference and counter-transference within relationships. *Transference* refers to the tendency of individuals to try to make current relationships 'fit' with the dynamics of previous relationship experiences. Being aware of this in a social work context is useful for practitioners in considering their own responses and most crucially unlocking knowledge about the experiences and behaviours of service users. *Counter-transference* refers to the reciprocal nature of relationships. In the context of the social worker–service user relationship, the social worker may respond emotionally in ways that provoke anxiety or discomfort within them. If such emotional behaviour is unpicked and examined, then the social worker has the opportunity to gain insight into previously unconscious emotional drivers and in turn feed the knowledge of this back into their interactions.

The impact of social context and associated cultures and norms (Turner and Stets, 2005) was noted earlier in the chapter. It is the apparent marginalization of these wider influences that is a weakness when applying psychoanalytic perspectives. Bower (2005) noted that issues of power, coercion, and organizational structures must be included in any analysis of a social worker's behaviour and role. John and Trevithick (2012) note that current conceptions of relationship-based practice integrate the inter- and intra-personal aspects within the wider context in which practice takes place. In terms of the conceptual framework proposed in this chapter, unconscious emotional drivers are an important part of a broader conceptualization of emotions.

John and Trevithick (2012) suggest that genuine relationships require the unconscious emotional elements to be brought to the surface. This will addressed further in the next section, which looks at emotional intelligence and the need to tune into the emotional worlds of service users, while simultaneously acknowledging and managing one's own emotional responses. In terms of the conceptual framework of emotions, psychoanalytic theory reminds us that the elusive unconscious aspects of emotions are no less pertinent in our interactions and behaviours, and lay the foundations for the need for reflection and supervision.

Emotions: emotional intelligence

The construct of emotional intelligence has taken different forms since the early 1990s. Emotional intelligence has caught the eye of academics, professionals, and the general public and is often cited as a positive attribute of any skill set. It may be that the wide-ranging benefits and outcomes that it is claimed are linked to the possession of emotional intelligence underpin this popularity. This creates an inclusive and aspirational concept that can be applied and targeted across a variety of contexts and socio-economic groups. The global appeal of the concept clearly has its roots in the notion that emotions are a universally experienced phenomenon (Darwin, 1890; Ekman and Friesen, 1971; Lazarus, 1991; Turner and Stets, 2005). It could be argued that this is in part reflected in the broad range of literature that has emerged, including that on leadership skills (Lindebaum and Cartwright, 2011), educational attainment (Goleman, 1995), nursing (Cadman and Brewer, 2001), and social work (Morrison, 2007). If we consider the afore-mentioned neurological studies of Damasio (1994) and LeDoux (1993) regarding the impact of neurological damage and its specific impact on emotional regulation and cognition, while IQ remains constant, we can further stake a claim for emotional intelligence representing a distinct construct.

Mayer et al. (1990) suggest that emotional intelligence consists of an individual's ability to be aware of their own emotional reactions to various stimuli and their abilities to manage their responses to such stimuli. They suggested that this balance of awareness and control allows individuals to make decisions with increased clarity and confidence. In addition to this self-regulation and awareness in relation to reaction and response to stimuli, they suggested that an ability to identify emotional responses in others is a key aspect of emotional intelligence. These abilities are further linked to an individual's communication skills and facility for empathic understanding. It is from these attributes, it is argued, that positive relationships and outcomes flow (Lishman, 2009). Goleman (1995) suggests that the attributes proposed by Salovey and Mayer (1989–90) help to explain why individuals who do not score highly on measures of IQ may still achieve more from a professional point of view than those with high IQ scores. This emphasizes the interpersonal aspects of what contributes to successful relationships that underpin wider activities such as employment. Put simply, emotional intelligence provides greater depth to how an individual may perform and in turn affects our understanding of what may contribute to actions and outcomes.

Voices of practitioners: John, a social worker for adults with learning disabilities

'I find emotions are of most use in empathizing with service users. Often people within social services find themselves in situations that they cannot see a way out of and the strain this places on them is evident. I feel that appropriate use of emotional intelligence in recognizing this helps build a relationship with the service user. I do not allow my feelings to dominate interactions (though they are not entirely absent) with service users, as I view my role as a professional one. This distance is required, particularly when difficult, and sometimes conflicting, decisions have to be made. It also serves to ensure that the service user knows throughout any interaction where they stand.'

John provides a vivid example of the importance he places on the management and control of emotions in his practice. He locates this within his professional role as a social worker and also notes the impact this can have on the relationships he forms with service users. It is important to note that John does not deny the presence of emotions and raises the role of empathy, which we will pick up on in Chapter 2.

Morrison (2007) provides a very persuasive link between emotional intelligence and social work practice. At the heart of his argument is the relationship between the intra- and inter-personal aspects of social work. This re-emphasizes the links between internally experienced emotions and the presentation of them externally. What is crucial about Morrison's thinking, and the concept of emotional intelligence more broadly, is that individuals can manage their own emotions and tune into the emotions of others to help develop positive relationships. Ingram (2013d) made clear the useful synergies between emotional intelligence and the hallmarks of relationship-building, and this will be returned to throughout this book, as it gives emotions a purpose and use in practice.

Emotions: conclusion and conceptual framework

In this chapter, I have reviewed key elements from the literature pertaining to emotions. It is evident that the topic of emotions has engendered interest and debate across the centuries and more recently from a range of research perspectives. Despite differing emphases and angles of approach, current understandings of emotions are accepting of certain key facets (Barrett, 2012).

From a sociological viewpoint, Turner and Stets (2005) include five key elements within their conceptual framework: biological, social context, labelling, expression, and appraisal. From a psychological perspective, Strongman (1987) finds space in his conceptual framework for the following elements: physiology, cognition, subjectivity, expression, consciousness, and unconsciousness. From a social psychology perspective, Zapf (2002) noted that emotions are subjective, physiological, and expressive. From a cognitive neuroscience perspective, LeDoux (1997) includes seven key elements: physiology, neurology, cognition, appraisal, context, experience, and expression. Finally, considering emotions from an expressive perspective, Kennedy-Moore and Watson (1999) noted the following elements: physiological arousal, subjective felt experience, and expression.

In the context of social work and this book, there is much to draw upon from the afore-mentioned conceptual frameworks (not least the synergies between them) and the literature reviewed in this chapter. The following areas noted in Figure 1.4 contribute to the underpinning conceptual framework of emotions in this book:

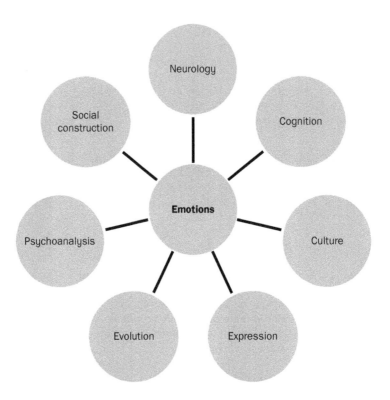

Figure 1.4 A conceptual framework for understanding emotions based on (Ingram, 2013a)

Key learning points

- The contribution from neuroscience discussed in this chapter highlights the important role of the brain in providing immediate responses and secondary processes of reasoning and cognition. These processes involve the appraisal of both physiological symptoms of arousal and an assessment of cues and context from experience.
- Emotions arise in response to significant events and stimuli. The meaning and significance that we attach to these events are crucial in determining both felt and expressed emotions. These judgements are in part an internal process based on conscious personal scripts and constructs, and unconscious memories and evolved responses. These responses are also influenced, directed, and constrained by wider social norms, cultures, and expectations that impact on the perceived significance of events. The outcome of such judgements will determine subsequent actions and behaviours.

- Emotions also have an expressive aspect. They are inter- and intra-personal phenomena that are expressed and displayed between people. Such expressions of emotion also sit within a wider context of influences, which can, to a certain extent, determine what is perceived to be appropriate, purposeful, and expected. Within this, there may be divergence between internally experienced emotions and those that are expressed. This socially constructed viewpoint is tempered by an acceptance that emotions, both unconscious and conscious, are inherently individual phenomena and are characterized by subjectivities and meanings within the private world of the individual.
- In the context of this book, the preceding cornerstones of the conceptual framework will also be considered in relation to the construct of emotional intelligence. This will allow emotions to be linked with greater clarity to the awareness, management, attunement, and empathic aspects of the social work role. It will act as a means of locating emotions within a pro-active relationship-based paradigm, yet with recognition of the wider professional context in which social workers operate.

This conceptual framework represents a theoretical and definitional underpinning for this book. It will be referred to as 'the conceptual framework' throughout and elements of it will be used to clarify and explain themes as they arise. This conceptual framework will sit alongside and interact with your own experiences and perspectives regarding emotions, and it is this relationship between knowledge, self, and practice that is at the heart of the book.

Further reading

Howe, D. (2008) *The Emotionally Intelligent Social Worker*. Basingstoke: Palgrave Macmillan.
David Howe provides some very interesting theoretical links between emotions, professional practice, and how emotional intelligence may have a positive role to play.

Turner, J. and Stets, J. (2005) *The Sociology of Emotions*. New York: Cambridge University Press.
This book is a very readable and thorough exploration of the psychological and sociological perspectives that underpin current and historical research on emotions.

2 Locating emotions in the context of social work

Chapter objectives

This chapter will:

- Establish links between the conceptual framework of emotions proposed in Chapter 1 with social work practice.
- Encourage you to consider your awareness of emotions within yourself and others.
- Highlight the debate about the emotions and rational decision-making and the impact this has on the perceived validity of emotions in social work practice.
- Place emotions within the context of care ethics.
- Introduce key themes relating to emotions and social work (i.e. professionalism, relationship-based practice, and reflection).

Emotions and social work: setting the scene

If we consider the messages contained within Chapter 1 that show our emotions to be an essential element of who we are as human beings, then it is clear that emotions should play a pivotal role in social work practice. Given the impact that emotions have on behaviour, attention, decisions, appraisal, and motivation, emotions must be a central driver behind the actions of social workers across the myriad of contexts and situations in which they operate. Furthermore, if we accept that our emotional worlds give meaning to our experiences and relationships with others, then we can begin to see that they form a significant part of the toolkit of a social worker when establishing relationships with service users, colleagues, groups, and communities. Finally, our awareness of the rules, norms, and cultures that impact on the way emotions are interpreted and expressed requires social workers to engage in significant reflection and analysis of the opportunities and challenges associated with the recognition and use of emotions in social work practice.

It might be surprising to note that despite the overwhelmingly self-evident importance of emotions in all aspects of our lives, their place within social work is at times obscure, contested, and most certainly uncomfortable. It is this rather murky relationship that gave rise to this book. Ingram (2013a) found that social workers were divided in terms of the applicability and desirability of emotions within their practice. The 'battle lines' were drawn around issues such as professionalism, rationality, relationships, empathy, decision-making, defensibility, risk, quality of supervision, and organizational culture. These will be introduced in this chapter and examined in depth elsewhere in the book. In a nutshell, emotions have often been pushed to the sidelines due to lack of knowledge or clarity about their role. Chapter 1 has established a conceptual framework to address the rather nebulous nature of the emotions. This is not to suggest for a moment that references to emotions are absent from social work literature, rather that they are often subsumed into broader topics such as reflection, skills, stress management, and personal/professional perspectives. In recent years, there has been an upturn in the literature focusing on relationship-based approaches to practice, and in particular the need for the awareness of the emotional worlds of oneself and others to engage in effective relationship in practice (Hennessey, 2011; Munro, 2011; Ruch, 2012; Ingram et al., 2014). Recent writings on relationship-based practice often cite the rise of bureaucratic and managerial approaches to practice as being the catalyst behind it. In some sense, it is about reclaiming the importance of the people (social workers and service users) within the processes and procedures that provide the framework for practice.

The aim of this chapter is to help you think about your own emotional world and how it impacts on your practice as a social worker. It will come as no surprise for me to reveal a strongly held belief that emotions are at the heart of what is to be a social worker and to practise as a social worker. This belief underpins this chapter and provides a guiding ethos for the remainder of the book. I will use a case example and a series of learning activities to help you to engage with these ideas and begin to cast a light on your own emotional world and how it is engaged or constrained by your experiences in practice.

Case study

Lorna is in the first year of a three-year undergraduate social programme. She has completed her first semester, which consisted of campus-based lectures and tutorials. As she embarks on her second semester, she is excited by the prospect of embarking on her first experience of practice learning. Lorna has very limited experience of working with people, having come straight into the course from school.

The first month of the semester focuses on 'preparation for practice learning'. This will entail a range of groupwork projects and role-play activities to help Lorna begin to develop a sense of her current skills, values, and attitudes in conjunction with a range of practice contexts and scenarios. This is a significant change from her first semester, which had a strong academic focus in terms of studying and essay writing.

Lorna feels rather vulnerable in appearing to be lacking in knowledge and experience. She is also wary of saying the 'wrong thing' in groups, which may make her come across as judgemental or naïve. She is being asked to think about 'who she is' and to examine her value base. This is entirely new to her and she privately resents having to talk about this sort of thing and would much rather go back to the lectures, studying, and reading.

Learning activity

- Do you have experience of thinking and learning in the way that Lorna is being required to do? Why do you think social work programmes include such elements?
- Why do you think that Lorna may be feeling uncertain about this new way of learning and thinking? Does that resonate with your experiences?
- What support could/should Lorna receive from her peers and academic staff to allay her concerns?
- What are the potential risks of Lorna entering a practice learning opportunity without beginning to reflect on her emotions, experiences, and 'self'?

Getting to know you: a good starting point

In Chapter 3, we will look more closely at the role of reflection and its role in helping social workers to unpick the complexities of the emotional content of their practice. Reflective practice involves active thinking about what social workers bring to specific situations in terms of knowledge, experience, values, and skills. This self-knowledge is then examined in relation to the presenting features of any given practice context. This allows social workers to begin: (1) to understand what they did and why they did it, what informed what they did and understood about a situation, and what others might think about the situation and their actions; (2) to evaluate how effective their practice was; and (3) to consider how this would impact on any future practice (Ingram et al., 2014). This very brief account of a reflective process is replicated in various forms across the vast body of literature concerned with reflection. What unifies the plethora of models of reflection that you will come across is the need to develop a sense of what motivates, drives, informs, and underpins our decisions and actions in practice. Put simply, you need to develop a sense of 'self'.

Anecdotally, I am conscious that within every cohort of students there will be those who find reflection a difficult, awkward, and at times embarrassing process. Part of this is likely to be to do with the need to reveal thoughts and feelings, which ordinarily are kept private and seldom examined. I have also heard students talk about reflective activities as a 'hoop to jump through'. This perspective would appear to be underpinned by a disconnection between the process of reflecting and the practical impact on subsequent practice and decision-making. This book is about making the links between our emotional worlds and the more visible and tangible world of practice. Trevithick (2005) notes the importance of shining a light on *intra*-personal knowledge in order to inform and support our *inter*-personal practice. Hennessey (2011) argues that the fusion of these two spheres is the basis of what it is to operate in a relationship-based manner. Hennessey (2011) uses a lifeline approach to encourage social workers to examine their previous experiences and how these contribute to how we perceive the world and drive our decision-making and approach to relationships.

In this chapter, I use a lifeline approach but with a particular focus on emotional awareness and the potential impact on practice. This will then allow you to approach the subsequent issues and debates in the chapter (and the rest of the book) with a developing and ever-evolving sense of your own emotional self.

Before you engage in the following task, I would like to provide a few tips to help you get started and also highlight potential pitfalls that may inhibit you (and in turn undermine how you engage with the content of the book). The good news is that what you include in your 'lifeline' can be kept for your own private use. This is not to say that discussing such issues with others is not of merit, but simply that it removes a very common block for social work students and practitioners. I would encourage you to be unconstrained in terms of what you identify as being of relevance. Too often participants are directed towards deaths, births, and life transitions. These may be pivotal for you, but equally it could be something relatively fleeting such as the loss of a favourite possession or the response to a new culture while travelling. The other important thing to note is that you can edit, delete, and amend as you go, so nothing needs to be permanent. You may find it interesting if you reflect on why you are changing or reprioritizing certain events. The most important thing to know about lifelines is that they are continuously evolving and there is no such thing as perfect self-knowledge. What you produce today will be the start of a process. Analysis of your lifeline should continue throughout your career as a social worker, and it will be constantly affected by new events and your own evolving understandings, contexts, and perceptions.

Learning activity

- You will need a large piece of paper (preferably A3). Draw a line from one side of the paper to the other. The starting point will be your birth and the end point is today. It is useful to divide the line up into years. This will help you visualize the time span and also stop you running out of room. Start at any point along the line and begin to note significant events in your life (Figure 2.1).
- On a separate piece(s) of paper, you should then consider the following questions in connection with the 'events' identified:
  - What made this event significant for you?
  - What are the key features of the event: who was there, what happened?
  - What emotions did you experience at the time? Why do you think that was? How do you now feel about it? If your emotions have changed, what contributed to this change (this often alerts you to other significant events)?
  - How might others involved have perceived the event?
  - How might this impact on your practice? Can you identify an emotional response that may occur in practice due to this (i.e. fear, attraction, anger, avoidance)?

If we consider Lorna's situation above, it is likely that she will be somewhat overwhelmed when confronted with a sheet of paper that is blank other than an apparently meaningless line. If Lorna is encouraged to identify whatever comes to mind and then examine it, this may help her to avoid feeling that there are no events in her life that have been of significance. Hypothetically, Lorna may remember a time when she forgot her lines in a school show. Her analysis could look like the following:

- What made this event significant for you?
  It was very embarrassing because I went bright red and I knew my parents were disappointed that I had made a mess of it. My friends laughed at me and it was talked about for ages afterwards.

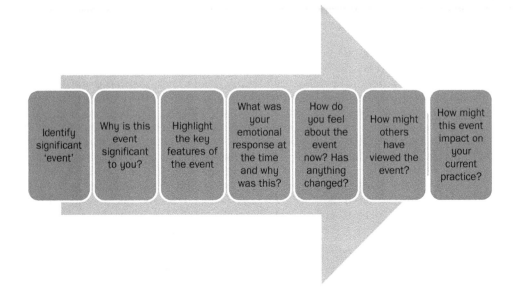

Figure 2.1 Exploring significant events based on (Houston, 2012)

- What are the key features of the event: who was there, what happened?
  All the parents of the class were in the audience as well as all the other pupils. When it came to my lines, my mind went blank, I stuttered, and had to just say 'sorry' and hope that someone else spoke to fill the silence.
- What emotions did you experience at the time? Why do you think that was? How do you now feel about it? If your emotions have changed, what contributed to this change (this often alerts you to other significant events)?
  I remember feeling extremely scared and anxious with my heart beating fast and my head feeling dizzy. I had not really prepared well and that coupled with the pressure of everyone looking at me pushed me over the edge. I still feel a bit nervous when I think about it. I don't really feel too differently about it, as I have been very successful at avoiding such circumstances since. I still feel very anxious and red if I ever have to speak out in class.
- How might others involved have perceived the event?
  I think people probably felt sorry for me and relieved it wasn't them. I felt that they thought I was stupid at the time.
- How might this impact on your practice? Can you identify an emotional response that may occur in practice due to this (i.e. fear, attraction, anger, avoidance)?
  I am dreading having to do presentations to my class group or contributing to meetings when I go out on my practice learning opportunity. I don't want to fail due to falling apart in a meeting. I wonder if I really need to speak in large groups because I am fine one-to-one and that is what social work is all about.

The example above shows how an event in our past can influence our emotions, decisions, behaviours, and efficacy some time after they occurred. For Lorna, it is clear that there is a potential for avoidance of speaking in large groups. This has the very real risk of undermining her ability to represent service users in many forums and in turn compromise the outcomes for them. It would also appear to be tied up with a fear of fail-ure and not meeting perceived expectations. Such self-awareness can begin the process of deepening one's understanding of how emotions impact upon us. Lorna may be able to identify other events in which she has shown confidence (she already identifies a strength in a one-to-one setting), which will help her to manage and contain her emotions more easily. Furthermore, if she reflects on her feelings of anxiety and disempowerment in large groups and meetings, she may be able to reflect upon how such forums are experi-enced by services users. This in turn could lead to more insightful support and empathy within her practice. This example thus underlines how self-knowledge can help us iden-tify the sources of our actions and perceptions, and in turn allow us to manage our emo-tions when they may be detrimental and draw directly upon them when they can help us to practise effectively. It also illustrates why lifelines are a useful tool to use with service users to support them to gain greater clarity about their own lives and experiences.

'Emotions versus reason' and 'relationship-based practice versus rational-technical approaches': debates, overlaps, and solutions

The title of this section purposefully uses the word 'versus' to underline the tendency for these core debates to be seen in a binary fashion with little room for compromise or com-patibility. As you proceed through the chapter and the rest of the book, it will become clear that these debates are much less clear-cut and that both sides have much to offer. Indeed, having considered the role of cognition and appraisal of emotions in Chapter 1, it is clear that the judgements we make about events and the way we interpret, categorize, and prioritize these judgements are rooted in neurological and experiential processes (Ingram, 2013b). That is, emotions and thoughts are inextricably linked rather than being in some way at odds with each other. The balance between the relationship-based aspects of social work practice and rational-technical approaches mirrors much of this debate, as it is concerned with the compatibility (or otherwise) of the apparently fluid and subjective aspects of relationships and the more concrete and predictable aspects of the procedures, knowledge, and processes that characterize the latter approach.

Emotions versus reason

It might be useful at this stage to gain some clarity around definitions before examining these debates in more depth. In Chapter 1, we examined the concept of emotions and noted that emotional responses provide individuals with signposts to attach meaning to events and situations. Rosenberg (1990) notes that emotions are *thought* about, and cog-nitive processes that draw upon previous experiences, cultural cues, and subconscious triggers and drivers underpin our sense of self (Fridja, 1988; Lazarus and Lazarus, 1994; Searle, 2010; Barrett, 2012). Reason and rationality, however, have a pronounced focus on logic and concrete factual evidence (Forgas, 2001).

Ingram (2013b) notes that the apparent uneasy relationship between emotions and reason is reflected in familiar informal discourses. Consider the following statements:

Don't let your heart rule your head.

I think he was just too emotional to think straight.

She is letting her emotions get to her.

I need to keep my head clear.

These are statements that we will all likely recognize from conversations and literature. They all point to the potential contamination by emotions of clarity and thought, thus creating a perception that emotions are potentially unruly and undesirable, and best marginalized, removed or controlled. If we accept these at face value, then it is easy to see why social work has often looked to tightening procedures and emphasizing the use of evidence to underpin decision-making and minimize the risk of poor practice (Rustin, 2005). Such messages provide the backdrop to the context in which you will approach this book and how social workers try to explore the debates about emotions and decision-making. Howe (2008) and Forgas (2001) note that such messages reverberate throughout history and can be found in the works of Plato, Kant, and Descartes. Such views have been challenged, however; for example, the Enlightenment philosopher David Hume argued that emotions and reason are able to work in harmony (Howe, 2008). Indeed, Barrett (2012) notes that the history of research into emotions is marked by a constant (and unhelpful) quest to create barriers between those who believe emotions to be cognitive, neurological, physiological or socio-cultural. Barrett argues (as I have in Chapter 1) that these perspectives combine to constitute a broad and inclusive concept of emotions.

If we return to the case study above, we see that Lorna may be struggling to manage some of these culturally nuanced debates about the appropriateness and relevance of

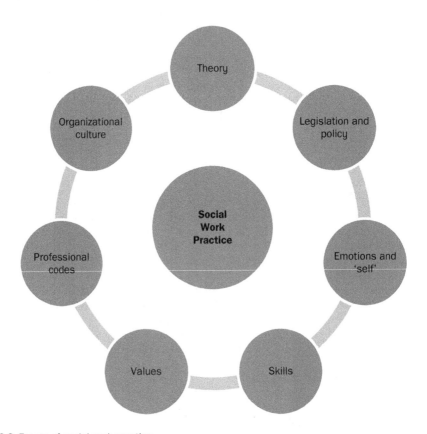

Figure 2.2 Facets of social work practice

emotions in decision-making. Her first semester will have required her to write essays, drawing upon theory, research, legislation, and policy. She may have become familiar with terms such as 'what works', 'defensible decision-making', and 'evidence-based practice', which suggest that her practice can be determined by a clear body of knowledge. The sense of disjuncture and discomfort that she feels as she enters the practice learning part of her programme, is in part rooted in the need to acknowledge that the concrete and rational elements are something she brings to help guide her practice alongside the intrapersonal qualities and skills she will bring to bear within her practice. She may be struggling with having to give up the security and certainty of theory and knowledge as articulated in academic essays. This combination of factors helpfully illustrates the compatibility of emotions and reason rather than them being at odds (Figure 2.2).

Relationship-based practice versus rational-technical approaches

The debate as described in the title of this sub-section is of course rather crude. However, the rise in interest in the centrality of relationships within social work practice has been explicitly identified as a reaction to the perception that social work has increasingly moved in a direction that emphasizes the role of rational-technical features such as procedures, policy, and guidelines (Munro, 2011; Ruch, 2012; Ingram, 2013c; Ingram et al., 2014). We will examine the role of emotions and relationships in much more detail in Chapter 4; however, it is important to gain a sense of these issues, as they are a core aspect of understanding how emotions can contribute to social work practice.

Ingram et al. (2014) helpfully conceptualize the two sides of this debate as 'hard' and 'soft'. The hard features refer to theory, research, procedures, and legislation, while the soft features refer to emotions, values, relationships, and reflection. They argue that these two sets of features are ever present and are essentially interlinked. Munro (2011) notes that in recent years the role of relationships and the information generated through the associated interpersonal dynamics and encounters has been replaced by an emphasis on what she describes as the 'conscious, cognitive elements of the task' (p. 86), which are associated with procedures and information recording. Whittaker (2011) states that this can drive a wedge between these two facets of practice and leave the relationships vulnerable and less valued.

Learning activity

- Based on your experience, how are the two sides of the aforementioned debate balanced in your practice?
- Are you given space and time to develop relationships with service users?
- Do you have the opportunity to consider your emotional responses to your practice?
- What are the merits, in your view, of a rational-technical approach?

Ferguson (2005) noted that a succession of high-profile child death reviews had been characterized by an increasingly rational-technical response. That is, tightening procedures and reducing the autonomy and subjectivity of individual judgement would be the best means of averting such tragic circumstances in the future. This of course echoes our previous discussion about the notion that emotions may be an unwelcome variable when making clear and defensible decisions. Ferguson challenged the wisdom of such shifts in emphasis and powerfully brought the emotions and psychological facets of the Victoria Climbié case back into view, and in turn noted the potential opportunities and benefits for social workers (with support) to explore and use their emotional responses to inform decision-making and professional judgement. Rustin (2005) stressed that to neglect such exploration of emotions risks an indecisive and compromised approach to decision-making. If we return to the conceptual framework in Chapter 1, what Rustin (2005) is highlighting is that our emotional responses to situations and relationships form a cogent and powerful stream of information to guide us.

It may appear from the preceding discussion that there is a gap between professional guidelines, codes, and polices and the role of emotions and relationships in social work practice. However, this is emphatically not the case and there are many examples of autonomy, use of self, relationships, and values. For example, the Professional Capabilities Framework (PCF; College of Social Work, 2012) highlights the need for social workers to engage in critical reflection and analysis, and that practitioners must take cognizance of factors such as relationships, ethics, and use of self. The PCF makes explicit mention of the notion of emotional resilience and the need for social workers and social work students to consider their well-being in relation to their practice. The British Association of Social Workers' Code of Ethics for Social Work (BASW, 2012b) also makes clear the need for reflection and thinking ethically about relationship-building in practice (Ingram et al., 2014). The Munro Report (Munro, 2011) is explicit in its assertion that social workers need to be allowed greater autonomy, and that they should be permitted and supported to explore the complex emotional aspects of their practice. The Social Work Task Force report (DCSF, 2009) echoed these themes and highlighted the role of high-quality supervision to facilitate the effective use of self and autonomy in relationships in practice. This is extremely helpful, as it recognizes the need for organizational and professional support for social workers to achieve effective autonomy rather than it simply being located within the individual him- or herself.

If we briefly return to the case study, it is clear that Lorna is right to be sensing the tensions and debates involved, and the need to consider her use of self and how this impacts on the relationships she makes and the associated decisions and actions that arise from these. However, she will also be able to turn to the documents above (which is not an exhaustive list) to see that the 'hard' and 'soft' elements of practice *are* present and correct in the codes and guidance that underpin the profession. Grant et al. (2014) note that social work education must also respond to the need to consider emotional resilience and awareness if graduates are to be equipped to manage these aspects of their professional role and profile. They surveyed a significant number of social work programmes in England, and the aspects of the curricula that met this need included topics such as reflective writing, role-play, supervision, and practice learning. This highlights that Lorna is at a point in the programme where she is being required to engage in the 'emotional curriculum' envisaged by Grant et al. (2014).

Emotions and practice: bringing the strands together

Hopefully, the preceding discussion will have made a strong case for avoiding the continued use of the word 'versus' when thinking about emotions and social work practice. I have already noted the need for high-quality supervision to facilitate reflection and self-awareness among social workers (DCSF, 2009). Beddoe (2010) notes that when this is absent and supervision and support are dominated by a rational-technical approach, social workers simply suppress or avoid engaging in such analysis. Given the centrality of emotions in terms of directing our attention and judgements, this would appear to be a rather worrying scenario (Ferguson, 2005; Ingram et al., 2014).

Voices of practitioners: Grace, a children and families social worker

'I had a mother who was verbally abusive and physically intimidating towards me, threatening to "get me". This caused me a lot of fear in regard to my own personal safety and anxiety regarding my assessment. "What if I've assessed the wrong thing." I was very anxious about meeting her and her partner again and wanted to constantly put it off, which would not have been in their children's best interests.'

It is clear that Grace has taken the fear she has felt when engaging with this family and moved it beyond simply recognizing the emotions. Grace was then able to consider the impact that these emotions may have on her ability to be clear in her assessment and also the potential they may have for triggering avoidance of the family. She is right to contextualize this within the notion of the children's best interests and this will hopefully be a key source of information for her when working with the family. Grace stated she would not write about these emotions in reports, despite the significance to her practice, but did identify supervision as a key forum for exploring such issues. I will discuss forums such as supervision in much more detail and the written recording of emotions in later chapters.

Holland (1999) examined the factors that social workers appear to base their decision-making on, and suggested that social workers often depicted themselves as neutral observers who readily distance themselves from the process of decision-making. In a sense, the social workers in Holland's study reported a scientific approach where decisions around risk were presented as clear calculations rather than infused with their own interpretations and emotions. In a survey of social workers about the role of emotions in their practice, Ingram (2013a) found that most respondents felt that emotions *were* a key aspect of being a social worker, but that they felt that they could remove emotions from decision-making. This is an interesting point, as it would seem to contradict what we know about the dominant role of emotions in helping us understand and find meaning in situations. What would seem to be at play here are the strong professional/cultural cues about what constitutes valid decision-making. Ruch (2012) argues that while managerialist approaches to social work would suggest that decision-making can be reduced to something that is relatively simple and process-driven, the reality is actually much more emotionally laden and complex.

In essence, the inclusion of emotions is social work discourse is ultimately about permissions, safety, and organizational culture (Ingram et al., 2014). The vast body of research surveyed in Chapter 1 suggests that the central role of emotions in how we make sense of the world and our relationships is inescapable (Barrett, 2012). If we consider the impact of professional norms on how workers may present their emotions (Hochschild, 1983), we can begin to recognize that there may be a gap between what social workers identify as important in their decision-making and what actually guides their decision-making. The opportunities for social workers to recognize, articulate, and use their emotional responses will be dependent (in part) on the support and supervision they receive. We will examine these themes of supervision and organizational cultures in Chapters 6 and 7.

Voices of practitioners: Rachel and Simone

Rachel: *'I am not aware that my personal emotions do impact on my practice, as I believe I am able to remain objective whilst being able to show empathy.'*

Simone: *'Anxiety is my way of knowing that there is something that is not quite right about a situation – this has naturally led me to be more curious perhaps and ask more questions – generally there are further concerns that are only uncovered by asking the right questions.'*

Rachel stated from the outset that she could remove emotions from her practice. Rachel's answer raises some key issues about the place of emotions in relation to practice and empathy more specifically. She felt unable to give an example of the positive impact of emotions because she felt there simply was no impact due to her removal of emotions from the process. The use of the word 'personal' is an interesting one, in that it highlights something distinct and potentially detached from the professional. The other interesting part of the response is her view that empathy and removal of emotions are compatible.

Simone's response contains an example of the active use (as opposed to removal) of emotions. She contends that her emotional response (anxiety in this case) impacted on the direction of her assessment and provided motivation to ask particular questions. Simone goes on to provide a very vivid concept in a later question in the survey when she states:

'The practitioner needs to be able to apply a set of "professional emotions" to these situations – being over-emotional is not professional, practical or helpful, however neither is cutting yourself off from your feelings . . . There needs to be a balance – practitioners need to be educated about healthy exploration of their own emotions.'

The idea that there is something that could be described as 'professional emotions' is a fascinating idea. For the purposes of this chapter, it is useful because it opens the door to considering emotions within the professional sphere and highlights the complexity of this. There are interesting links here to emotional regulation in terms of the use of the word 'over-emotional'.

The familiar debate about boundaries between personal and professional spheres is less applicable when talking about emotions, as emotions are intrinsic to being *human* rather than being a social worker.

Positive emotions and social work

When one thinks about emotions and social work, it is easy to dwell on the complex emotional responses that arise when working with people experiencing difficulties, crisis, and trauma. Ingram (2013a) found that the majority of the social workers he surveyed viewed emotions through the lens of stress and coping rather than considering the full range of emotions that includes happiness, satisfaction, and joy. Indeed, Pooler et al. (2014) cite the shock at seeing the word 'joy' and 'social work' linked together as the catalyst behind their interest in the area. This is extremely important for this book also, as our conceptual framework of emotions encompasses the full spectrum of emotions rather than creating a hierarchy that prioritizes certain types of emotions. This of course means that the lifeline proposed earlier in this chapter should (indeed, must) include events that elicit positive emotions. It is through such self-awareness that confidence and resilience can be sought and achieved (Pooler et al., 2014).

Writing generally about positive emotions, Fredrickson (1998) notes that one reason why negative emotions gain greater attention is that they are often linked more explicitly to associated actions. In the case study above, for example, Lorna's feelings about presenting in public (fear) are clearly linked to a related behaviour (avoidance). If Lorna had been happy to speak in public, the associated behaviour (willingness) would be less active and visible. Fredrickson suggests that a greater appreciation of the role of positive emotions can have a powerful impact on behaviour and performance. This would seem to be a useful signpost for social work, as it may reduce the reticence about articulating emotions and/or citing them as drivers of behaviours. For example, the emotion of 'interest' inspires investigation rather than fear, which can narrow our attention (Fredrickson, 1998). This could potentially have a powerful effect on practice if social workers were supported to acknowledge such emotions. Isen et al. (1987) note the ameliorating effects that positive emotions can have on negative ones and the potential for a positive cycle of emotions to emerge. In Figure 2.3, we can begin to visualize such a process in a social work context. What is powerful about the cycle depicted in Figure 2.3 is the recognition that the highly charged emotional world of social work is not necessarily beset with negativity, but that the opportunity to name and explore emotions is the key to their management and use.

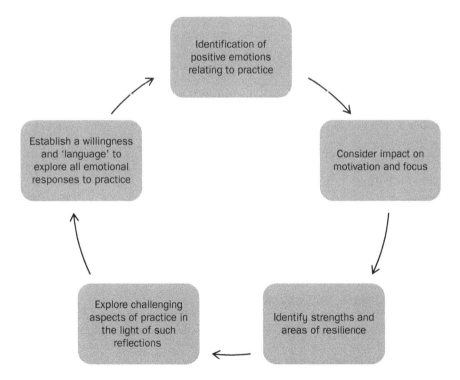

Figure 2.3 Building upon positive emotions in social work practice

Pooler et al. (2014) note that it is rather ironic that a profession that places significant emphasis on strengths-based approaches with service users should struggle to incorporate them into thinking about their *own* practice experiences. Pooler et al. set out to determine which aspects of the job gave rise to feelings of joy. The sources of joy and satisfaction for social workers included:

- Making a difference to the lives of service users.
- Working with a service user group that you are committed to.
- Making connections and relationships with service users and colleagues.
- Gaining perspective about one's own life.

This is a highly instructive list because it gets to the heart of why people become social workers. I have asked first-year students at the start of their social work programmes 'why they chose social work as a profession'. Without fail the answers include 'helping others', 'making a difference', 'being a people person', and 'I want to work with a particular service user group'. What is interesting is that they directly map onto the findings of Pooler et al. (2014). This suggests that the core motivations to become a social worker are directly linked to the positive emotions experienced in practice. This is a further argument for claiming congruence between the transformative relationship-based aspects of practice and the professional identity of social workers.

Kinman and Grant (2011) note the importance of building emotional resilience and cite reflection and support as a way of maintaining a positive perspective for social workers. By broadening this out to positive emotions, exploration of emotions can help maintain a sense of role and celebrate the positive aspects of the profession. Collins (2007) talks of how optimism can be nurtured through the identification of strengths and positives in supervision. If we consider the anxiety felt by Lorna in the case study, it may be that a focus on her original motivation to become a social worker coupled with acknowledgement of the strengths that guided her through the student selection process would unlock her anxiety about reflection and thinking about herself. Perhaps she would also be able to locate the triggers and drivers behind her motivation to become a social worker within her lifeline. This again underlines the need to think of such reflective and analytical tools in a positive light rather than to primarily focus on difficulties and negative emotions.

Learning activity

- What are/were the motivating factors for you to choose social work as a profession?
- How are these motivating factors rewarded by engaging in practice?
- Do you find it easier to explore positive or negative emotions?

Emotions, social work, and ethics

A key challenge for social workers is the need to do what is ethically 'right' in their practice. Webb (2001) suggests that social workers should have an 'ethical will' to achieve the best possible outcomes for service users. Stanford (2010) rightly notes that there are many competing factors that impact on this, and one that is associated with managerialist working cultures is the fear associated with 'getting it wrong'. This places social workers in a difficult position, and one in which they may wrestle with their own emotional responses to a situation and the competing emotions about 'what if they make the wrong decision?' It is in this complex arena where social workers can point to their professional codes or practice codes of practice (SSSC, 2003; CCW, 2004; NISSC, 2004; BASW, 2012b), which set out an ethical framework and purpose for the profession. The central tenets vary slightly by regulatory body but most often include:

Social service workers must:

- *Protect the rights and promote the interests of service users and carers*
- *Strive to establish and maintain the trust and confidence of service users and carers*
- *Promote the independence of service users while protecting them as far as possible from danger or harm*
- *Respect the rights of service users while seeking to ensure that their behaviour does not harm themselves or other people*
- *Uphold public trust and confidence in social services*
- *Be accountable for the quality of their work and take responsibility for maintaining and improving their knowledge and skills.*

(SSSC, 2003: 3)

Kant (1785) suggests that deontological approaches to actions rely on following moral rules. The codes listed above are in essence the moral rules that underpin social work and in turn impact on the way workers practise and feel about their practice. Critics of deontology point to the lack of flexibility and the omission of the wider pressures and influences that may guide actions, and indeed the individual interpretation and commitment to moral rules. Keinemans (2014) notes that traditionally emotions have been seen as an impediment to moral judgement. However, Keinemans goes on to state that our knowledge of the neurology of emotions suggests that the process of appraisal is effectively instantaneous and it is alongside this that we subsequently apply moral and ethical reasoning. Pizzarro (2000) further stakes a claim for the role of emotions in ethical decision-making by noting that emotional responses are rooted in reality and experience and as such are a culturally and morally nuanced phenomenon (Turner and Stets, 2005). They help us to decide what is the morally right thing to do by giving us signposts to previous experiences and understandings of situations. Indeed, Keinemans (2014) notes that concepts such as social justice are rather static (and have little meaning) without being understood on an emotional level to help us to make judgements and identify situations where we need to respond or prioritize.

Houston (2012) points to *virtue ethics* and *care ethics* as being congruent and helpful when considering the blurred aspects of social work relationships, use of self and practice. Virtue ethics refers to one's approach coming from one's own character and being. This relies on a social worker's ethical approach being intrinsic to him or her. This requires self-knowledge and ongoing reflection and supervision to foster and manage it. This chimes well with the aforementioned need for social workers to reflect upon the emotional drivers that underpin their motivation to become social workers, in order to gain the confidence to trust and use these drivers when making judgements and decisions in practice. The opportunities for social workers to benefit from such nurturing supervision are variable (DCSF, 2009; Ingram, 2013a), which may compromise a virtue ethics approach in certain circumstances. This may reduce the willingness and 'safety' for workers to develop the kind of autonomous practice purported by Munro (2011).

Care ethics is a relationship-based ethical approach that places an emphasis on actions being guided by the views and needs of the service user. This places a strong emphasis on the fruits of positive relationship-building, and recognizes and harnesses the importance of the intra- and inter-personal aspects of these relationships. Sevenhuijsen (1998) identifies two key aspects of care ethics: the rational/cerebral (head) aspects of relationship-based ethics and the emotional and empathetic (heart) elements. This is helpful because it firmly establishes that care ethics does not simply rely on the fluid emotional worlds of the social worker and service user, but that it resides within a context of knowledge, rules, and norms. This echoes the social constructed aspects of emotions presented in Chapter 1, which add depth and meaning to our emotional responses (Turner and Stets, 2005). Houston (2012) suggests two further aspects to the construct of care ethics: the practical approaches adopted by social workers (hands) and the motivation that workers have to care (feet). The construct so created notes the impact of relationships on the actions and approaches taken in practice but also brings us back to consider the core drivers for being a social worker. There is also an important congruence between the qualities that service users desire of social workers and a care ethics approach. For example, qualities such as empathy, genuineness, warmth, and motivation are recurrent themes that emerge in the service user literature (Lishman, 2009). These will be picked up in more detail in Chapter 4. Care ethics is a useful contribution to this book, as it creates an ethical space for social workers to disentangle the complex location of emotions within their practice.

By returning to the case study to consider a role-play scenario that Lorna has to complete with a volunteer service user as part of her preparations for practice, we can begin to illustrate how this might be applied. Let us suppose that the basic premise of the role-play is that Lorna is to meet with a 15-year-old who has been absent from school for some time and the young person is at a point where they wish to go to college but are still struggling with behavioural problems. Lorna may well feel rather overwhelmed in terms of how to approach the situation, as this is early in her programme. Box 2.1 helps show how a care ethics approach can be utilized.

Box 2.1: Head, heart, hands, and feet

Head: draw upon knowledge of developmental theory, social exclusion, and policy to gain a theoretical understanding of presenting issues and consider her statutory role.
Heart: establish a trusting relationship characterized by empathy and a willingness to work with potential resistance. Genuinely commit to seeking the views of the young person.
Hands: recognize the high levels of motivation and clarity of goals the young person has. This will lead to the selection of a task-centred approach.
Feet: reflect upon the emotional drivers that underpin Lorna's desire to become a social worker to encourage her to persevere and become aware of power and respect.

It is evident from this simple example how powerful a tool such an approach can be and how, if given the opportunity to engage in such thinking about oneself and one's practice, the connections between the 'hard' and 'soft' features of practice (Ingram et al., 2014) can be intertwined with a sense of self and a commitment to ethically sound practice.

This brings our discussion back to the key theme of this chapter – that emotions are congruent and intrinsic to the decisions and actions that social workers make in practice. This mirrors the central role that emotions have in guiding and informing the decisions made and actions taken by humans in all aspects of their lives. To suggest that social workers are able or willing to avoid emotions seems fanciful and rather odd. It would be much more useful if we accept and acknowledge their role so that we can gain greater insight into our own behaviours and judgements and those of others.

Learning activity

Choose a piece of social work practice that you are or have been involved in. If you are not yet at the stage of undertaking practice learning, you may wish to use a hypothetical case scenario encountered during academic study.

List all the ideas you can generate under the headings 'head', 'heart', 'hands', and 'feet'. Try to identify which elements are linked to your emotional responses; your internal drivers; the service user's views; theory, policy, and legislation.

Key learning points

- For social workers to effectively engage with the emotional aspects of their practice, they need to work to achieve a clear sense of the sources and impact of their own history. This is an ongoing process of reflection and analysis that is intended to lead to an awareness and *use* of emotions in practice.
- The familiar and historical debates around the impact of emotions on rational thought and reason were explored and compared in relation to similar debates about relationship-based practice and rational-technical conceptions of social work. It was argued that our knowledge of emotions research coupled with a clear sense of the professional purpose of social work suggests that emotions and professional decision-making are inextricably linked. It was argued that for decisions and actions in social work to be fully informed and effective, these 'hard' and 'soft' features need to be acknowledged.
- The place of emotions and use of self within a range of professional narratives and codes was identified.
- Positive emotions are highlighted and it is argued that these have a powerful role in directing practice and establishing a sense of efficacy and resilience.

Further reading

Ingram, R., Fenton, J., Hodson, A. and Jindal-Snape, D. (2014) *Reflective Social Work Practice*. London: Palgrave Macmillan.
This book takes a very practical approach to looking at reflection. The 'hard' and 'soft' elements of practice discussed in this chapter are introduced. Readers are encouraged to consider their emotional responses to practice.

Ruch, G., Turney, D. and Ward, A. (eds.) (2010) *Relationship-based Social Work: Getting to the heart of practice*. London: Jessica Kingsley.
This is a very readable collection of chapters that guide you through the central themes relating to relationship-based practice. The book is also realistic and recognizes the other factors that contribute to the decisions and actions of social workers in practice.

3 Reflection and the exploration of emotions

Chapter objectives

This chapter will:

- Highlight the central role of reflection in social work in supporting and developing informed and self-aware practice. Reflecting upon one's emotions is important in order to recognize, manage, and use them effectively.
- Introduce a range of approaches to reflection to support its use in practice.
- Present a dramaturgical approach to thinking about practice that is intended to bring together the inter-personal, intra-personal, cultural organizational, and professional strands of practice.
- Examine the concept of emotional intelligence in the context of reflective and reflexive practice.
- Identify the benefits of engaging with emotions and reflective practice.

Reflective practice and emotions: setting the scene

The first two chapters of this book have highlighted the interconnectedness of emotions and thought. The conceptual framework proposed in Chapter 1 notes that emotions have an important role in directing our attention and providing meaning to situations and relationships. That is, emotions help and prompt us to think, analyse, and draw upon previous knowledge and current cultural cues. In its very simplest definition, reflection is the activity of *thinking* about events that are (or may be) of significance to us (Rosenberg, 1990). You will already be familiar with the concept of reflection, as it is the cornerstone of social work programme curricula and literature. The many useful texts on reflection propose a range of approaches that transform the concept of reflection into a purposeful and effective process. In this chapter, I will highlight a selection of approaches to reflection and although this will not be exhaustive, it will serve as a springboard to the broad range of reflective practice literature (Schön, 1983; Moon, 2004; Ingram et al., 2014).

I use the word 'purposeful', as reflection involves examining one's emotions, values, assumptions, and knowledge in relation to an event with the core purpose of achieving greater insight into and understanding of one's current and future actions (Fook and Gardner, 2007). The Professional Capabilities Framework (PCF; College of Social Work, 2012) identifies critical reflection as a key domain of the framework and in turn the role that reflection has in achieving effective practice. This brings us to the notion of *reflective practice*, which highlights the throughput of the aforementioned thinking and analysis into ongoing practice rather than it being a detached cerebral process. The word *critical* is often used in conjunction with reflection. White et al. (2006) state that for reflection to move into a critical sphere, it requires an acknowledgement and integration of wider contextual influences, such as organizational constraints and political discourse, into the analysis of one's individual actions and beliefs. Figure 3.1 highlights the key aspects of critical reflection proposed by White et al. (2006).

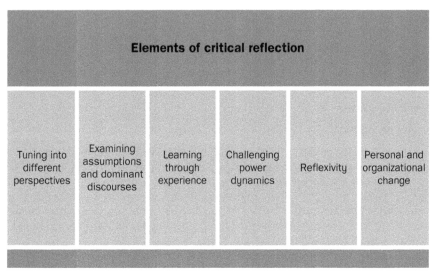

Figure 3.1 Elements of critical reflection
Source: Based on White et al. (2006)

Ingram et al. (2014) highlight that by adopting a critically reflective approach that includes consideration of the factors illustrated above, social workers can engage in a learning process that will allow them to view their practice through the lens of others and provide them with a platform to change aspects of their practice and challenge individual and organizational dynamics that may be oppressive or obstruct positive outcomes for service users. This brings us to the concept of *reflexivity*, which is commonly used alongside and in place of the term reflection. Reflexivity can be defined as the ability to consider how our values, emotions, beliefs, culture, and experiences combine to influence our actions and judgements. This in many ways expands the concept of reflection to uncover aspects that are not immediately apparent within a given situation (Fook and Gardner, 2007). Holmes (2010) suggests that reflexivity allows individuals to bring together the psychological and sociological facets of our 'self'. This echoes our conceptual framework in the sense that our emotions can only be fully understood by examining their origins not only in terms of our individual experiences but also in terms of the wider cultural norms and context (D'Cruz et al., 2007; Barrett, 2012).

The importance of the role of reflection has been prompted by the inherent messiness and complexity of social work practice (Yip, 2006). Yip uses the metaphor of the layers of an onion to illustrate the process of uncovering the individual, organizational, political, and societal factors at play in any given practice situation. Yip notes that such a process requires social workers to explore their emotional responses to their practice and potentially uncover previously subconscious emotional markers, which can be identified and understood in terms of their meaning and impact (Ferguson, 2005; Ruch, 2012). If we think back to the conceptual framework in Chapter 1, we can see that this depth of reflection is necessary if social workers are to truly engage with the breadth and depth of their emotions, and in turn avoid their suppression or marginalization.

The chapters in Part 2 of this book contain many explicit and implicit references to reflective practice. For example, Chapter 5 highlights the reflective process undertaken when social workers prioritize and edit the information they record in writing about their practice. It is noted that this process is in part intra-personal and related to individually held values, emotions, and knowledge, but also is constrained and facilitated by wider factors such as professional role and organizational culture. This echoes the work of Ingram et al. (2014), which states that the social work landscape in inhabited by both 'hard' (legislation, theory, policy, professional frameworks) and 'soft' features (values, emotions, and relationships). Meaningful reflection must incorporate all these elements to achieve a critical and useful outcome.

Case study

Malcolm is a social worker in a community social work team for older people. He has worked in this team since he qualified as a social worker 5 years ago. He chose this context of practice because he is passionate about actively seeking the views of older people and making their voices heard in the decisions that impact their lives. His passion is in part based on witnessing what he viewed as rather dismissive and de-humanizing practice in a residential care home for older people during a practice learning opportunity while training to become a social worker.

His team have seen many changes in recent months, which has included him changing supervisors three times in quick succession. This has been rather unsettling for Malcolm, as he values the opportunity to reflect on the dynamics of his practice and the balance between limited resources and trying to achieve positive outcomes in partnership with service users. It has also been a very difficult time personally for Malcolm because his mother died two months ago following a long illness. His mother's physical health and mobility deteriorated significantly in her final months and Malcolm fought hard for her to remain in her own home until the end of her life. This was at odds with his sister's (Joyce) desire to move their mother into a residential nursing home in order for her to receive as much care and support as possible. This difference in opinion has led to an ongoing dispute between Malcolm and Joyce. Joyce holds the view that her mother's death would have been preventable had she received the care package that she had proposed. Malcolm has not been able to resolve this issue with Joyce and it is a source of stress and anxiety at a time when his workload is increasing due to staff shortages.

One of the cases that Malcolm is currently involved in concerns a home care assessment for Arthur. Arthur is an 82-year-old man who lives on his own in a first-floor flat. He has suffered from arthritis for many years, but recently this has started to have a significant impact on his mobility and ability to undertake household tasks such as cooking, cleaning, and self-care. Malcolm feels a strong connection with Arthur and has established an open and positive relationship with him. Malcolm's recent personal experiences are affecting his confidence in the judgements he is making in this case.

Learning activity

- Can you identify any issues that Malcolm would benefit from having the opportunity to engage in further reflection on? Make a list of the factors you think might contribute to a critical approach to such reflections (i.e. power, resources, etc.).
- If Malcolm does not have an opportunity to engage in reflection, what might be the implications for his work with Arthur?

Reflective practice and emotions: an introduction to models and methods

The literature relating to reflection has mushroomed since the early 1970s and there is a dizzying array of models and approaches that one can select to guide and underpin one's engagement with reflection. In some ways this is positive, in that it underlines the importance of reflection for practitioners and enhances the likelihood of finding an approach that is a 'good fit' for you as an individual. However, it can also create uncertainty about the efficacy of differing approaches, and can result in a closed approach to reflection where tried-and-tested methods are held onto due to the seemingly unfathomable array of alternatives. I cannot cover the vast range of reflective literature here, and instead try to make it more approachable and make explicit links to the roles of reflection and emotions.

Models of reflection: an introduction

Ingram et al. (2014) note that there are three key types of reflective models: the *cyclical* approach, the *list* approach, and the *phased* approach. In many ways, these conceptions of reflection have much in common (with similar goals) but have different emphases in terms of focus, content, and process. We will consider each type of model in turn and provide a link to the case study to highlight how they might be used in practice. These case study examples will focus on Malcolm's uncertainty about the impact of his personal experiences on his professional judgement.

Kolb (1984) is credited with the best-known of the *cyclical* models. Cyclical models guide the individual through a process of undertaking an activity (practice), reviewing this experience, identifying key learning points, and then feeding this back into practice. This is a familiar definition of reflection and if used in conjunction with this book, one could choose to focus on the emotional elements of a situation. This element of choice has underpinned the criticism Kolb's model has received, in that it is perhaps too basic and the efficacy of such an approach is subject to the rigour and quality of what individuals bring to it. Gibbs (1988) developed the cyclical approach to incorporate emotions and make explicit demands on the individual to consider how they felt at the time and the impact that this may have had on their decisions and actions. This links well with our conceptual framework, in that it recognizes the links between emotional responses and subsequent appraisals and actions.

Learning activity

Malcolm will be prompted by such a model to acknowledge his assessment of Arthur's needs as a significant event. By using Gibbs' (1988) model, Malcolm will be asked to consider his feelings in relation to this event. This may lead him to explore his feelings about his mother's circumstances, but equally may lead him to simply explore his feelings of uncertainty and frustration at a surface level without unpicking its sources. Depending on the quality of this analysis, Malcolm will develop a new understanding of his practice and he will then be able to translate this into subsequent actions.

- What qualities would Malcolm's supervision arrangements require to allow him to engage in meaningful reflection?
- What does the above example suggest in terms of the limitations of such a model of reflection?

The *list*-type models are built on a series of questions or steps that are intended to guide participants' thinking and focus. This prescriptive approach can be seen in the models proposed by Johns (1994) and Ash and Clayton (2004). These models are attractive, as they direct participants to ask specific questions and acknowledge the enormity of what is potentially being asked within a reflective process. By this I simply mean that participants benefit from a clear direction and focus from the outset, rather than being confronted with a cyclical model which demands a greater degree of autonomy and choice of focus. Lay and McGuire (2010) build on the DEAL model (Describe, Examine, and Articulate Learning) of Ash and Clayton (2004) and require participants to integrate the personal and academic content of their thinking and to identify how these facets interact. This is very helpful when thinking about emotions and social work, as it directly connects emotions to the choices and preferences we have in terms of theoretical explanations and requires us to unpick the sources of our actions and decisions. This has much in common with the notion of Socratic questioning techniques (Goleman, 1995; Barsky, 2009). This approach has its roots in the teaching of the early Greek philosopher Socrates, and emphasizes the need for learners to articulate their thinking in a manner that explores and highlights the foundations of assumptions and decisions. In its purest form, the supervisor would take the stance of someone who knows 'nothing' and who requires the social worker to provide all the information about a situation. An example of this might include a series of questions such as:

- What do you mean when you say you made an assessment of risk?
- Can you give me another example to illustrate this?
- Why is assessing risk important?
- What are the assumptions about the importance of assessing risk?
- Is there another way of thinking about risk?
- Why did you come to your conclusion about the level of risk?
- How did you feel at the time of making the judgement?
- What caused you to feel that way?
- Is there an alternative explanation?
- What would others think about your judgement? Why do you think that is?

This type of approach to questioning may seem rather laborious at a glance, but is very useful if a reflective process is to enhance our self-knowledge and our understanding of how we arrive at the judgements that we make in practice. We can see here an explicit move towards reflexivity in the sense that the basis of our judgements and emotional responses is unpeeled layer by layer (Ingram et al., 2014).

Learning activity

If Malcolm's supervision is characterized by a list-type approach, he will be given a degree of scaffolding and direction to his thinking. This may allow him to consider the interaction between his personal circumstances and his professional judgements. He may also be able to shed light on the origins of his judgements and allow him to connect elements of his value base such as a commitment to respect and self-determination. This may help him understand the motivators behind reaching certain judgements and indeed how he selects and edits the information that feeds into them. The depth achieved here will be dependent on the quality of the relationship with his supervisor and the nature and focus of the steps/questions contained within the model adopted.

- How 'safe' would you feel in exploring the type of Socratic questions noted above? What circumstances/environment would be conducive to such an approach?
- Apply/adapt the Socratic questions to a practice context of your own.

Ingram et al. (2014) see *phased* approaches to reflection as being particularly useful when seeking depth and unpicking the assumptions that may lie at the heart of our practice. This pushes reflection much more firmly into an arena of learning, and requires the space, time, and safety to engage in an unfolding process. Taylor (2010) proposes the REFLECT model of refection, which consists of the following:

- **R**eadiness – this refers to the need for participants to have the time, space, and environment to engage in meaningful reflection. This ties in with the aspiration of the Social Work Reform Board to secure high-quality supervision for social workers.
- **E**xercising thought – the opportunity to take a step back from actions and decisions in practice and consider what informs these.
- **F**ollowing systematic processes – utilize processes, steps, and questions to direct and focus one's reflection and analysis.
- **L**eaving oneself open to answers – this emphasizes that a reflective process should not have a premeditated conclusion or 'right' answer. Rather, one should be open and secure enough to accept and welcome unexpected outcomes and self-knowledge.
- **E**nfolding insights – the need to be 'held' during the process. This echoes the need for social work supervision to allow containment as new understandings emerge (Ruch, 2009).
- **C**hanging awareness – this recognizes the aforementioned purposeful nature of reflection in that such depth of reflection must not be simply a therapeutic process (although this is an important aspect) but one that feeds explicitly back into subsequent actions.
- **T**enacity – a recognition that the process of reflection requires effort and persistence to achieve results.

This type of model is useful in that it fuses a rigorous list-type approach with a clear process. It is particularly useful when considering the role of emotions in social work practice, as it pays cognizance to the *experience* of undertaking a critical approach to reflection and the vulnerabilities and uncertainties that are inherent in exploring and analysing the conscious and subconscious aspects of our lives. It also makes clear the responsibilities of the supervisor and/or organization in terms of the conditions and skills that they must offer such a process. These points will be picked up in more detail in Chapters 6 and 7, as such depth of reflection is a significant undertaking (Yip, 2006; Ruch, 2009).

Learning activity

If such an approach is adopted in supervision for Malcolm, then he will be able to approach the task of reflection without having a preconceived outcome. Malcolm may be able to consider the nature and significance of his personal circumstances for his practice. This may highlight the usefulness of harnessing such emotional responses to direct his interest and motivation to ask questions and seek information. Once the drivers behind his judgements are identified, then an ongoing examination of the components of his decision-making can be undertaken so that his practice is enhanced and informed. This emphasizes the cyclical and ongoing nature of reflection and, if Malcolm is well supported, should lead to an increase in self-knowledge and emotional resilience.

- What are the factors that would contribute to your 'readiness' to engage in such levels of reflection?

Reflection: methods of recording and engagement

In Chapter 6, we will consider a range of opportunities for reflection, including supervision, self-reflection, peer support, and mentoring. Supervision is perhaps the most familiar forum in which to engage in reflection about one's practice. This forum lends itself to a verbal narrative approach to reflection, with the social worker verbalizing their thoughts and responding directly to questions and prompts within a one-to-one interaction. This is true to an extent, but it would be remiss to neglect the potential for other methods of reflecting and in turn recording the fruits of reflection. In many ways, this echoes the preceding introduction to reflective models, in that there is scope for individual social workers to identify approaches that suit their learning styles and the context in which they practise.

The following list is intended to provide an overview of some of the key methods that you may wish to consider when engaging in reflective processes and activities:

- *Reflective journals*: As the title suggests, these are inspired by a traditional diary format, which provides physical and reflective space for an individual to record thoughts about practice on a daily/weekly basis. These can be 'shaped' in different ways. Bassot (2013) provides a useful framework that helps structure one's entries (an echo of the 'list' approach) to encompass emotions, theory, role, and relationships. This form of written reflection may be for private use or for sharing with others. Lomax et al. (2010) note that a key benefit of this approach is that it creates a recorded history of one's thinking and development. However, it could be argued that the process of and permanency of putting one's thoughts down in writing inhibit openness and increase potential vulnerability (Healy and Mulholland, 2012).

- *Visual mapping*: Moon (2004) and Lomax et al. (2010) note the usefulness of developing visual maps of one's reflections. This may suit some learners more than others, but visual mapping allows one to see clearly the connections between such factors as emotions, theory, practice, and legislation. This helps direct further reflection and may uncover previously unknown links and connections.
- *Poems, photographs, and metaphors*: This allows one to engage in thinking and analysis in a way that may be less daunting and direct in some circumstances. Moon (2004) suggests that such techniques can then serve as a stepping-stone to more explicit applications to practice situations.
- *Dialogue*: As noted above, this is often seen within the context of supervision. Ingram (2013c) found that social workers valued the opportunities to engage in reflection informally with their peers. Interestingly, this was seen to benefit from *not* being recorded, hence allowing experimentation and exploration within a 'safe' environment. It was also noted that such informal dialogue was often available 'on the spot' and lent itself to the busy and fluid nature of social work practice.
- *Video and audio*: This can involve the recording of a reflective dialogue (i.e. supervision) to enable better analysis of one's responses and presentation, or can involve (where appropriate) the analysis of actual practice. Such approaches can be very powerful but can also feel over-powering and invasive. There is a need to consider individual learning styles as well as issues of confidentiality.
- *Self-reflection*: This in many ways can involve some of the methods listed above, but emphasizes that it can take place within a private sphere. This benefits from the reduction of external pressures to present in a particular manner (although one should not under-estimate the potential for avoidance and deception within ourselves) due to others and can be the key opportunity to reflect following an event and/or within it (Schön, 1983).

This list illustrates some of the ways that the preceding models may be conducted and recorded. The appeal of these methods will vary according to the individual and the context in which they find themselves. What is important is that one is constantly seeking ways to engage in reflection and drawing from this broad pool of approaches. This should help avoid the potential for reflection to become routinized and stagnant.

Reflection and emotional intelligence: positive outcomes

In Chapter 2, we explored the importance of developing a keen sense of 'self' and in turn being able to understand, manage, and use our emotional responses to situations that arise in social work practice. The models and approaches to reflection presented above sit very comfortably with the concept of emotional intelligence. Mayer and Salovey (1997: 5) propose that emotional intelligence is 'the ability to perceive emotions, to access and generate emotions . . . and emotional knowledge, and to reflectively regulate emotions so as to promote emotional and intellectual growth'. Goleman (1995) states that emotional intelligence is not a destination or a static quality that individuals may possess, but the product of an ongoing process that is constantly developing and evolving. This mirrors the ongoing nature of reflection, in that social workers are by definition thinking and reflecting about ever-changing fluid circumstances and relationships. Mayer and Cobb (2000) make links between emotional intelligence and leadership skills, stress management, resilience, and job performance. These potential benefits map well onto the aspirations of the PCF (College of Social Work, 2012) in terms of establishing a confident, informed, and reflective workforce. It is useful for us to establish the links between reflection and the five domains of emotional intelligence proposed by Salovey and Mayer (1989–90) (see Box 3.1).

Box 3.1: Links between reflection and emotional intelligence

- *Self-awareness*: understanding and recognizing why we have particular emotional responses to situations. This is central to the intra-personal aspects of reflection and the emphasis on how emotional intelligence can result in greater confidence in decision-making (Goleman, 1995), and links with the throughput of reflection into *reflective practice* (Ingram et al., 2014).
- *Managing emotions*: the ability to use this self-awareness to guide subsequent behaviours. This may be in accordance with specific cultural/social norms and roles, but also in terms of managing the dynamics of relationship-building (Schutte, 2001). This links with the relationship-based aspects of social work practice and the recognition that reflection allows these relationships to be located within the context of professional roles and responsibilities (Munro, 2011; Ruch, 2011).
- *Motivation*: emotional intelligence and awareness allow us to prioritize and respond to circumstances. This links with the purposeful nature of reflection in terms of influencing future practice, and also with the conceptual framework proposed in Chapter 1, which recognizes that emotions are linked to important behaviours in practice such as curiosity and avoidance.
- *Empathy*: the ability to tune into the emotional worlds of others (Goleman, 1995). This is enhanced by one's own self-knowledge and is at the heart of establishing trusting and genuine relationships (Hennessey, 2011; Howe, 2013). This links well with a key aspect of critical reflection and reflexivity, which is to consider the perspectives of others and how they may feel and perceive circumstances (Redmond, 2006; Ingram et al., 2014).
- *Relationships*: emotional intelligence is inextricably linked with human relationships (Goleman, 1995; Cadman and Brewer, 2001; Morrison, 2007; Ingram, 2012). Reflection in the context of social work is also by definition about the relationships that are established in practice and how these can be managed to achieve positive outcomes for service users (Hennessey, 2011).

Saarni (2000) identified the concept of *emotional competence* to be a key benefit that emerges from reflecting on one's emotional responses. Emotional competence is defined as the ability to use one's emotional awareness in relationship-building and social interactions. In essence, it is the confidence that flourishes through the development of self-knowledge. This may be manifested in empathy, emotional reciprocity, and congruence between actions and self. The need for reflection in social work is often prompted by the uncertainty that arises from the complex and difficult circumstances one encounters in practice (Hennessey, 2011). Ferguson (2005) suggests that where such opportunities for reflection are absent, then a sustained sense of uncertainty and anxiety can arise from relationships. This could be viewed as emotional *incompetence* in the sense that our emotional responses remain unknown or unexamined and in turn can push workers to seek comfort from rational-technical conceptions of practice in which there is a 'proper' way to act (Saarni, 2000; Ingram et al., 2014). Beddoe (2010) and Hafford-Letchfield (2009) note that this tendency to move towards a procedurally flavoured version of reflection from one which is critical and focused on learning and development is evident in social work contexts where the assessment and management of risk are a key feature. Ruch (2012) emphasizes that regardless of the opportunities for reflection available to social workers, the *reality* of practice remains and with it the complex emotional content therein.

John and Trevithick (2012) locate the benefits of reflection within a psychodynamic arena and note that the previously unconscious processes that influence our relationships can be identified and in turn fed into the way we practise in an informed and purposeful manner. Cornish (2011) states that this depth of reflection requires time and social workers need to be 'held' in the process rather than the emphasis being on a speedy identification of emotional drivers. This notion of being held (metaphorically) chimes with the seminal work of Bion (1962), who spoke of containment being the process whereby individuals (social workers in our case) are supported through a process of anxiety and uncertainty and given time to explore and reframe their understanding. Cornish (2011) and Ferguson (2005) note how patchy and vulnerable such opportunities for reflection are in social work, and also highlight how the absence of such opportunities can lead to the suppression of emotions and dangerous practice. These themes, which will be picked up again when we look at the role of supervision, support the call for reflection on emotions and the 'soft' features of practice to be safeguarded (Ingram, 2013b; Ingram et al., 2014).

A dramaturgical approach to emotions and social work

The idea that social workers 'present' themselves and their practice in ways that respond to and interact with the context in which they operate is a recurring theme throughout this book, and is a key aspect of the conceptual framework of emotions presented in Chapter 1. The importance of shining a light on all aspects of one's practice when engaging in reflection is crucial if an holistic and all-encompassing understanding of the complexities of social work is to emerge. This chapter has identified a range of 'topics' that might feed into whatever reflective process is adopted. The notion of the 'hard' and 'soft' features of practice proposed by Ingram et al. (2014) helpfully underline the interplay between intra-personal processes and concrete streams of knowledge such as theory. Holmes (2010) adds a further reflexive dimension in terms of the need to consider how important it is to consider other people involved in any situation and how the prevailing context and culture of the environment affect all parties involved.

It is likely that you have begun to visualize this list of topics and the temptation is to ensure that one works one's way through the list when attempting to engage in critical reflection. This unfortunately may have the effect of turning what are otherwise expansive and flexible models of reflection into an increasingly linear and checklist-type process. In a sense, the development of a 'list' offers a rather prescriptive process to follow from beginning to end. Turner and Stets (2005) build on the work of Hochschild (1983) by proposing a dramaturgical approach to thinking about context, behaviour, and emotions. The term 'dramaturgical' clearly has its basis within the sphere of *drama*. It allows one to consider the way people behave and feel within a metaphorical arena that takes the idea of 'acting' into the familiar context of theatre and stage. In a way, this allows one to provide a clear framework to take a step back and view the *social construction* of any given context of practice. It links conceptually to the notion that emotions are experienced, appraised, and expressed. Expression is the aspect that is particularly influenced by prevailing norms and cultures, yet the private and internal spheres of emotional experience are also at play. If we take this thinking as a starting point, we can begin to develop a fluid model that casts a light on the way social workers present themselves in different contexts. The emphasis is on developing a reflective and analytical narrative about one's practice. As one engages in deeper reflection, so the clarity and complexity of dramatic devices such as 'plot', 'characters', 'motives', and 'setting' emerge. Figure 3.2 highlights the key aspects of this dramaturgical way of looking at social work practice and emotions.

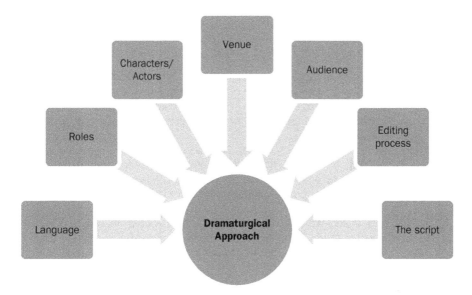

Figure 3.2 A dramaturgical approach to reflection on practice

Box 3.2 provides an illustration of this dramaturgical approach. If we link back to the case study and put ourselves in Malcolm's shoes, we can begin to see how he might be able to stand back from the perceived messiness of his practice and explore and reflect upon a range of pertinent features. Given the hypothetical nature of the case study and limited information contained therein, I will use my 'dramatic licence' to add more depth and detail to the case. The focus is on Malcolm as a social work practitioner and how he can reflect upon his emotional responses to practice within the context of wider influences and other perspectives.

Box 3.2: Dramaturgical presentation of social work practice

The script *Context*: Malcolm is involved in the assessment of need of Arthur, an 82-year-old who has been experiencing increasing difficulties connected to his arthritis. This has led to a need for increased (and fluctuating) levels of support for self-care and other domestic tasks. Malcolm is working alongside Arthur to assess the level and nature of support required, and consider whether this can be achieved within his home.

Plot: Malcolm has recently experienced the loss of his mother and has an ongoing dispute with his sister (Joyce) about the level of support his mother received in the final months of her life. Joyce argued for their mother to be moved into residential care, whilst Malcolm felt strongly that his mother's wishes to remain in her home should be honoured. This unresolved personal issue provides the backdrop to his assessment of Arthur and is coupled with a lack of available supervision to support Malcolm to examine his judgements. Arthur has stated (with the support of his daughter) that he would like to remain in his home if at all possible.

The venue(s)   1. The contact between Malcolm and Arthur takes place within Arthur's home. Malcolm is able to adopt an empathetic approach to his practice and is keen to encourage Arthur to be confident in expressing his views. Malcolm also seeks to identify areas of strength and resilience in Arthur.

2. Malcolm is required to feed back to a weekly resource allocation meeting, which looks at assessments across a range of cases and makes recommendations about which services are available for allocation. Malcolm must adjust his presentation in this forum, as he has to argue for allocation of scarce resources.

3. Malcolm also discusses this case in supervision. Due to the changes in his team, supervision has taken on a rushed and case-orientated tone. This means that Malcolm struggles to engage in reflection and is less certain about exploring the emotional content of his practice.

The actors   *Leading roles*: Malcolm, Arthur, Arthur's daughter, Malcolm's sister Joyce, Malcolm's supervisor, and members of the allocation panel.
Supporting cast: Malcolm's team and agency, Malcolm's caseload, Arthur's social network, and the local authority.

The language   Malcolm has to adopt a range of approaches to language according to context. For example, he is keen to avoid jargon and tries to speak in a warm and friendly manner to Arthur to help establish their relationship. He needs to articulate the reasons for his actions and recommendations to his supervisor. He also will need to present his assessment in a manner that is evidence-based and persuasive to the resource allocation meeting. He also has a supportive colleague at the next table with whom he often discusses how he feels about different cases.

The roles   Malcolm is a social worker for a community-based team for older people. He works with Arthur who has voluntarily sought assessment and support due to difficulties he is experiencing at home.

Malcolm receives supervision from his line manager who has a responsibility to oversee his caseload and support him as a member of staff. This has been inconsistent recently.

Malcolm also brings his 'self' into his practice, which is shaped by a range of factors including his own personal experiences and relationships. Most pertinent to this case is the difficult relationship he has with his sister Joyce.

The audience	For Malcolm, all the parties noted above form a part of the audience. Unlike the theatre, he 'performs' to these audiences separately and together at different times.
The editing process	Malcolm will adjust and edit his communication and recording in different ways. He will report to his supervisor what he feels to be the relevant points about the case. He will write a report that explains his view of the case and his recommendations to the resource allocation panel. He will also feed back to Arthur and his family his views of the situation at a range of points.

Box 3.2 presents the key elements of this particular case in a manner which Malcolm would readily be able to produce if given the permission and space to do so. This then serves as the starting point and map to proceed with reflecting on all aspects of the case and in particular the emotional and cultural drivers at play. The purpose of this approach is to locate the practice and the role of emotions within a clearer context. In isolation, it is difficult to ascertain why and where Malcolm's practice is influenced by different factors, or how he may choose to present his practice to others. Using this model, however, it is possible to see that his positive attunement to Arthur is a useful aid when engaging with him and establishing a relationship. The presence of influential frameworks such as the PCF (College of Social Work, 2012) provides an encouraging message about establishing open and positive relationships with service users to seek their views and is congruent with Malcolm's relationship with Arthur. This has direct links to the inter-personal aspects of emotions within the conceptual framework in Chapter 1, and the purposeful edge that emotions can have on our behaviour and the impact we wish to have on others. It is useful to consider, however, that the motivation to engage with Arthur (possibly rooted in his values and personal experiences) may have a direct impact (possibly at the expense of other people in his caseload) on his motivation to achieve positive results.

The relationship he is developing with Arthur may also be causing Malcolm a degree of anxiety, as he may be conscious that it mirrors that of his relationship with his mother. By laying out his practice in this dramaturgical manner, he can begin to see the interconnectedness of his personal and professional spheres. This may prompt Malcolm to consider the extent to which he is responding to the emotions generated by his relationship with his sister (hurt and frustration) within his practice. Is his motivation to achieve positive outcomes for Arthur or to achieve a sense of justification for his actions with regard to his mother? By unpeeling these layers, he may then begin to evaluate the extent to which he is genuinely 'hearing' Arthur's views. If emotions go unchecked, there is the potential for Malcolm to filter the information he receives to fit preconceived judgements and persuasions. This may then lead to a clearer sense of the sources of his actions in practice but also allow for links to his strongly held values around respect and advocacy.

A key strength of this dramaturgical approach is the emphasis on thinking about the different contexts and roles we inhabit within practice. This is crucial, as it reminds us that the emotional content of our practice is understood and presented in different ways depending on the context. Hypothetically, Malcolm may have met with Arthur on a twice-weekly basis and identified him as someone who would benefit greatly from home-based support and care. Malcolm would be required to articulate how he practised and how such recommendations and judgements were reached. He will have drawn on a range of what Ingram et al. (2014) would term 'hard' sources of knowledge within his practice that may have included theories of loss, social exclusion, and human development. As noted above, opportunities to reflect both formally and informally would allow Malcolm to examine his previous personal experiences and consider their impact on his appraisal and actions within the case. However, the *presentation* of his emotional reactions to Arthur's case may be very different within supervision, where it would need to be located in relation to his wider caseload and he may feel that the cultural cues in supervision require him to present an emotionally detached account of his practice. It is at this stage that Malcolm may need to seek a technical-rational interpretation of his practice at the expense of the emotional content and quality of his relationship. This would be even more the case when writing about Arthur in a report. This would require what Hochschild (1983) would term 'deep acting' in response to messages about what constitutes robust professional decision-making, but also 'surface acting' in that the omission of emotions from the report could be construed as an attempt to make people think you feel one thing when you actually feel another.

The focus of his supervision and the content of his reports might be linked to the aforementioned managerialist approaches to practice, which seek clear recordable and concrete processes and outcomes. This context pushes the drama and the 'plot' into places where it wouldn't otherwise have gone had Malcolm been given more consistent opportunities to explore and record the emotional impact of this case. It might be that the lack of consistent *formal* support will lead to a suppression of the emotional responses he is experiencing within his practice. To push this metaphorical model further, it is clear that the highly valued *informal* contact with his colleague constitutes a 'sub-plot', which helps to manage the disjuncture experienced by Malcolm when juggling competing pressures on the way he should act. This may be due to a less rational-technical culture to such discussions with peers. There is a dramaturgical edge to Goffman's (1983) 'model of interaction', and he helpfully suggests that the 'venues' that I propose are crucial in terms of *categorization.* Goffman suggests that we place environments into categories such as formal, informal, private, and fun in order to direct the way we present ourselves. Crucially, he emphasizes that such a view of interaction is cyclical, fluid, and bi-directional. In this sense, everyone involved in the case above (or indeed any social work case) are all actors responding to the rules, norms, and cultures of *their own* environment. This would suggest that Goffman's model is multi-directional in this case. In my view, this leads us back to an emphasis on the blurred human elements of social work practice and the implausibility of being able to reduce it to a technical-rational activity. This again is rooted in the conceptual framework proposed in Chapter 1, in that emotions are a core aspect of the ways in which we understand and act in response to events and stimuli. The danger of not recognizing this is that Malcolm may be forced to provide the equivalent of the fixed smile of a flight attendant (see Hochschild, 1983) rather than engaging in meaningful critical reflection to examine and explore the sources of and drivers behind his professional judgements. Put simply, adopting such a dramaturgical approach allows cognizance of the different ways in which we not only experience emotions but present and articulate them in relation to other people and environments. It is important to note that regardless of the environment in which Malcolm operates, the emotional labour involved in social work practice (and all aspects of his life) will continue: it is the presentation and articulation of these emotions that change.

The use of such a dramaturgical approach is in my view applicable to all the contexts of social work practice. Of course there will be differences in the cast members and associated plots, but the central focus on the social construction of emotions and how they are used and communicated will remain. Rosenberg (1990) notes the importance of reflexivity in terms of one's emotional responses to aid the development of self-knowledge and consequently inform one's actions. I would suggest that the dramaturgical approach illustrated above is useful as a *tool* to examine practice situations and encourage reflection in addition to its use as a way of unpicking the phenomenon of professional presentation.

In this chapter, I have made a case for the importance of reflection within social practice. Links have been established between emotions and reflection, although given the centrality of emotions to human experience, this is not a difficult connection to make. I have touched on the myriad of approaches and models and despite the differences between them, they ultimately act as a prompt and a framework to engage in thinking and analysis. The quality of the fruits of this reflective labour will be dependent on the individuals involved and the environment and culture within which they are located. These themes are threaded throughout the book.

Key learning points

- Reflective practice is the process in which social workers are given the opportunity to examine and consider the origins, meaning, and impact of their practice, which in turn informs subsequent actions.
- There is a plethora of models and methods to guide and support reflection. There are many synergies and overlaps between these; however, reflection requires purpose, direction, depth, and support to achieve meaningful outcomes.
- Reflection and reflexivity require time, space, and permission to explore the complex and uncertain aspects of practice. This requires an individual, organizational, and professional willingness to engage in the learning process without imposing any 'right' answers.
- Emotional intelligence and reflection have many overlaps conceptually and these links allow social workers to identify benefits for their practice, such as resilience, empathy, stress management, professional confidence, and self-efficacy.
- A dramaturgical approach to thinking about practice provides a framework to identify the key constituents of any given practice situation, and allows for a reflective analysis of how these factors interact and the role of emotions within this.

Further reading

Bassot, B. (2013) *The Reflective Journal*. Basingstoke: Palgrave Macmillan.
This very accessible book provides the reader with a plethora of tips and examples for engaging with reflective activities.

Yip, K. (2006) Self-reflection in reflective practice: a note of caution, *British Journal of Social Work*, 36 (5): 777–88.
This article identifies the strengths of reflective practice while placing it within a realistic context. Signposts to positive individual and organizational practice are provided.

Part 2
Applying and understanding emotions in social work practice

Part 2 of the book focuses on the practical application and examination of emotions in social work practice. The inter- and intra-personal aspects of developing effective relationships with services users are identified and the role that emotions and emotional intelligence can have within this process is highlighted. The role that emotions play within relationships is clear; however, the presence of emotions within the written articulation of practice is more contested and opaque. This is examined thoroughly and readers are encouraged to consider the ways in which the emotional content of their practice may be edited or ignored in writing, which in turn can compromise subsequent decision-making.

It is recognized that social workers require and seek support in a myriad of ways. The emotional content of practice should have a place within reflective and discursive forums such as supervision if the full depth and richness of practice are to be explored. Readers are encouraged to consider their own experiences, and the use of case studies throughout the book offers some examples and scaffolding to help facilitate this. The discussion is broadened out to consider wider factors such as organizational culture, managerialism, and professional narratives and how these impact on the place of emotions in social work. The final chapter pulls the key themes of the book together and proposes a model of a twenty-first-century social work professional that incorporates the explicit and essential contribution of emotions.

4 Engaging and communicating with service users and carers

Chapter objectives

This chapter will:

- Explore the concept of relationship-based practice and consider the importance of emotions within it.
- Establish links between the messages from service user-informed literature and the qualities and skills required of social workers.
- Highlight that empathy is a key facet of the social work 'toolkit' and assert the centrality of emotional intelligence and awareness.
- Identify the role that emotions can play in forming and guiding the use of skills when establishing relationships in social work practice.

Emotions and relationship building in social work: setting the scene

The first part of this book established a conceptual framework for emotions before highlighting how emotions can inform, guide, and contribute to social work practice across a range of contexts. It was also noted that once we explicitly incorporate emotions within our practice, we benefit greatly from the opportunity to reflect upon the sources and meanings of our emotions. This is in part about increasing self-knowledge and benefiting from the therapeutic aspects of gaining an insight into our experiences, but also taking this a step further and allowing the fruits of reflection to inform and direct our actions and decisions. Through such a process, the links between our emotional worlds and our relationships with others become purposeful and manageable.

In Chapter 2, relationship-based practice was shown to be key in highlighting the importance of emotions, and in many ways this chapter is the one where the place and importance of emotions can most intuitively be located. If we think for a moment about any of the significant relationships in our lives, it is likely that we will characterize and describe them in a way that links to our emotional responses. For example, if I think of close family members, a simple game of word association will produce a list that includes love, happiness, pride, fear, safety, and belonging. These emotional responses to close family are then linked to a series of behaviours that may include: motivation to be in regular contact; an urge to protect them from harm; a willingness to forgive; and a tendency to prioritize their needs over those of others. This rather simple example is useful in that it makes clear the links between emotions and the impact this has on the content, intensity, and quality of the associated relationships. This is not unique to friendship and kinship but also permeates relationships in all aspects of our lives (Barrett, 2012). Thus we can see the foundations of this chapter and the foundations of relationship-based practice emerging. It is this essential human connection between people that is informed, inspired, and appraised through our emotional responses. As noted in Chapter 1, these responses are rooted in previous experiences (both conscious and unconscious) and the prevailing culture/context, and the significance and meaning we attach to these will be inextricably connected to our emotional responses.

It is very common for people who aspire to become social workers to highlight their desire to 'help people' and 'to make a difference in people's lives'. These are so familiar that they may appear a little routine and trite, but that is to ignore the underlying emotional drivers that are at play. These altruistic statements are underpinned by our emotional responses and appraisal of the lives and experiences of others. These emotional responses are then filtered through a process that draws on cultural norms, personal values, and prior experiences to inspire and motivate actions. This leads social workers to commit to establishing meaningful and purposeful *relationships* with individuals in order to work in partnership to support them to manage and address difficulties and challenges.

This chapter emphasizes the role that emotions have in providing us with signals and signposts as we develop relationships in practice, however brief or sustained they may be. It is important to note that as soon as we move our discussion into an *inter*-personal sphere, a two-way process is involved where both (or indeed more) parties will be involved in appraising, using, and communicating emotions in order to build the blocks (or not) of a positive relationship (Ingram, 2013d).

Case study

Molly is a social work student on her final practice learning opportunity. She has been placed in a residential home for older people. The residents have a range of care needs and a key aspect of Molly's role is to establish relationships with residents and to seek their views to inform their care plans.

Molly was initially disappointed with this practice learning opportunity, as she felt that it was not 'real' social work and it wouldn't be challenging enough. However, within a few days of starting, Molly has become aware of the complexities of establishing relationships with older people with such varying needs, and has also become motivated by the challenge that it is presenting to her. Her practice educator gives her very positive feedback for her first reflective diary entry, which noted her complex emotional response (sadness, respect, confusion, empathy) to establishing a relationship with a resident called Helen who has very limited mobility and a deteriorating visual impairment. What has affected Molly most is the powerful and moving images of Helen and her family contained in the photographs around her room, and Molly's initial feeling of the distance between these images and Helen's present state.

Molly is encouraged to reflect upon the sources of her emotions and also the potential use these may have in supporting the development of her relationship with Helen.

Learning activity

- Think about a significant relationship that you have developed within a practice context. On a piece of A4 paper draw a line, with one end representing just prior to your first meeting and the other end being today (if the relationship is ongoing) or at the point you deem the relationship concluded. At different points along the line, list the emotions that you associated with the person and your relationship with them at that stage. It is important that you are honest at this point in the task and don't over-think it or tailor responses to what you think you *should* have been feeling. For example, you might have felt a degree of fear and anxiety prior to your first meeting due to information contained in previous case records. The task at this stage is simply to list the evolving emotions as your relationship progresses.
- On a separate piece of A4, replicate the timeline but this time note how you feel these emotions impacted on your ability and approach to establishing/maintaining the relationship. For example, it may be that you chose to meet the service user with a co-worker in the first instance and went armed with a set list of questions in order to maintain a sense of control and confidence.
- The key purpose of this exercise is to encourage you to establish links between your emotions and your actions. This will help you to identify the positive and negative impact that these emotions may have had on your relationship-building, as well as highlight just how central they are to the focus and quality of your practice.

Relationship-based practice and emotions

A relationship-based approach to social work is in many ways self-explanatory. It emphasizes the role and purpose of the relationship between worker and service user and highlights how the quality of this relationship can be the vehicle for seeking a depth of understanding and ultimately achieving positive outcomes. Phung (2014) suggests that it is the uniqueness of each individual's situation that pushes social work beyond a simple process of issue identification and solution. It is the perspectives and experiences of service users that provide a crucial stream of information and insight that provides signposts to 'solutions' or decisions rather than there being an 'off-the-shelf' remedy to hand for all cases.

How a social worker engages in a relationship-based approach is based on a myriad of models and methods, including crisis intervention, cognitive behavioural therapy, task-centred interventions, solution-focused therapy and counselling. This is important, as it marks relationship-based practice as an *ethos* of practice rather than a method. That is, it is an ethos that can underpin practice across all the contexts of social work practice, and the approaches and knowledge brought to bear on any given situation will vary accordingly within it. If we return to the learning task connected to the case study, we can begin to see that our emotional responses arise within our relationships and provide us with information and motivation to select particular approaches to those relationships.

The focus on relationships in social work is not new, and if we look to the seminal work of Biesteck (1957), we see that emotions were identified as salient aspects of the social work relationship from the outset. Biesteck talked about the need for emotional awareness, expression, and management within a relationship. In many ways, these qualities of a social work relationship mirror the key features of emotional intelligence discussed in Chapter 1 and underpin the links made by Ingram (2013d) to locate emotional intelligence within the skills and qualities required of positive relationship-building in social work. What is most important from the work of Biesteck is a resounding sense that relationships are important but also require specific and highly developed skills to underpin them (England, 1986). This links with the *professional purpose* of relationships rather than simply viewing them as indistinct from other types of relationships we may embark upon. Lishman (2009) highlights a range of qualities that underpin positive relationship-building in social work practice (Figure 4.1).

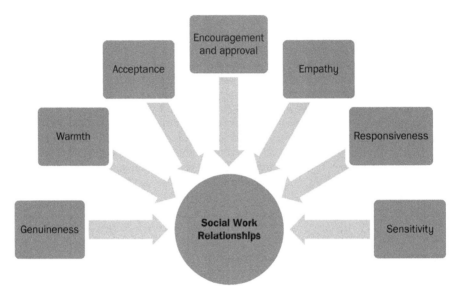

Figure 4.1 Qualities of positive relationships
Source: Based on Lishman (2009: 45)

These qualities map usefully with our conceptual framework of emotions. For example, the notion of 'warmth' requires a social worker to be able to manage their emotional expression in order to convey a sense of respect and engagement in their verbal and non-verbal communication. This requires emotional regulation and awareness to achieve this in the fluid and unpredictable arena of relationships (Howe, 2008). The importance of being responsive and sensitive is not simply about hearing what a service user tells us, but about really tuning into their emotional worlds and gaining a deep understanding of how they perceive and experience their lives. Only by thinking about emotions and their impact on our lives can we truly communicate sensitively.

It may be useful at this stage to make a link to the case study and consider how Molly may manage her emotions during the initial stages of forming a relationship with Helen. As noted in the case study, Molly felt a sense of disconnection between Helen as she is presenting within the residential home and the images of a younger person in the photographs in the room. If Molly recognizes this reaction, it may help her to consider the multiple losses experienced by many older people (Currer, 2007) and tune into a more holistic understanding of who Helen is in terms of identity and history. If Molly then deepens her reflection on these feelings, she may be able to see Helen also for who she is today with all her strengths, aspirations, and opportunities, rather than simply being 'stuck' with the emotional reaction of disconnection. Having engaged in this emotional thinking, Molly will be able to gain the confidence and motivation required to seek the views of Helen and begin to establish genuine understanding and empathy (rather than the sympathy that was evident in the initial emotional response). From this brief example, we can begin to see how emotions may open up our thinking about the relationships we form in practice and identify bodies of knowledge (loss theory and human development spring to mind here) to add meaning to our responses. In turn, this self-knowledge and emotional attunement will help us to engage meaningfully in relationship-building with service users (Hennessey, 2011; Ingram, 2013d).

Voices of practitioners: Megan, a children and families social worker

'I think there will always be individuals you have an affinity with and that is the danger of an emotional link with someone, and you need supervision to reflect on this . . . it is about the professionalism stepping in . . . I need everyone else treated fairly . . . I struggle with those service users who shout the loudest . . . often the most demanding and threatening get more time proportionally so it cuts both ways.'

Megan provides a useful pointer to the balance that needs to be struck between emotional responses to service users and the professional role. This returns us to that blurred area where engagement and being attuned are balanced by a need for regulation of emotions and a clear sense of role. This is a key area for discussion and the comments about supervision and individual/organizational responses to service users' differing visibility depending on their situation or approach are crucial.

Hennessey (2011) suggests three key components of effective relationship-based practice. These involve:

- *Use of self*: understanding where one's own emotional responses arise from and what circumstances trigger them is a crucial first step towards emotionally intelligent practice. Ward (2010) suggests 'self' refers to our beliefs, values, and emotions and how they interact with our environment.
- *Attunement to service users*: being able and motivated to tune into the emotional worlds of service users. This is not a passive act, but one that requires *communicating* empathy within the relationship.
- *Sustaining oneself and mindfulness*: effective relationship-based practice needs a significant degree of motivation and focus. This requires social workers to be able to manage their own emotions effectively and to be offered opportunities for reflection (i.e. supervision).

This list is useful, as it locates the conceptual framework proposed in Chapter 1 at the heart of relationship practice. For example, it emphasizes that emotional management and attunement are not simply 'natural' skills possessed by all social workers. It is not uncommon for social work students and social workers to view themselves as 'good with people'; this might be the ease with which one forms relationships and gains trust. What possibly underpins such qualities is an ability to manage one's emotions in order to facilitate focus and attunement to others. Given the components suggested by Hennessey (2011), it could be argued that in the context of social work, these skills need to be heightened in order to develop relationships in complex contexts while maintaining a professional role and purpose.

This slightly cautionary tone is intended to serve as a reminder of the complex issues that are often at play when a social worker and service user meet. By definition, there is (or should be) a clear issue or difficulty that requires the involvement of a social worker. This can lead to a myriad of potential relationship dynamics such as anger, distrust, fear, collusion, reliance, resistance, and compulsion. This reminds us that relationships and their associated emotional content operate within particular contexts and cultures. As discussed in Chapter 1, these differing contexts will affect the way we perceive and express our emotions (Turner and Stets, 2005). If we consider Molly's work with Helen, it is important to consider that Helen might potentially feel vulnerable within the environment that is the residential home. Perhaps Helen is unable to leave her bed without support and is reliant on significant levels of personal care. This may lead to a sense of loss of choice and control, which may feed into how she responds to Molly (regardless of Molly's intentions). This will require what Zirkel (2000) calls social intelligence to unpick how one's environment impacts on how one feels and relates to others.

Ingram et al. (2014) suggest that this contextual awareness is very helpful when establishing meaningful relationships in social work practice. Murphy et al. (2013) highlight these wider contextual issues as not just challenging but a fundamental block to achieving 'real' relationship-based practice. They argue that the Rogerian person-centred foundations of relationship-based practice are increasingly incongruent with the realities of statutory powers and bureaucratic priorities in social work. Murphy et al. suggest that if relationship-based practice is characterized by empathy, positive self-regard, and genuineness, there is a resulting tension with the presence of anticipated and desired goals associated with professional intervention. That is, the ability to be 'genuine' in one's relationships is compromised by having a specific professional purpose that drives the relationship. In a sense, the professional purpose is the reason for establishing the relationship rather than a genuine and unconditional desire to engage with another person. Murphy et al. (2013) go on to suggest that the ability to tune into and identify previously unknown feelings and perspectives within the service user may reflect a professional sleight of hand in that the trusting relationship is established with that purpose in mind. If we consider Molly, it could be argued through this lens that she is establishing a relationship with Helen with the purpose of assessment solely in mind. To an extent this is true, and it is a given of any positive social work relationship that there is a clarity of role and purpose from the outset (Trevithick, 2003). Additionally, Ingram et al. (2014) would argue that the keen awareness of the pressures and balances between relationships and statutory/professional requirements are present, *but* once identified can be managed and incorporated positively into one's practice. Indeed, Beckett and Maynard (2013) suggest that this professional role is (and must be) about going beyond simply being ourselves and is underpinned by professional values, theories, and codes.

Service-user perspectives: support for emotionally intelligent practice

A significant element of this book is concerned with developing arguments and justifications for the emotional content of practice to be included in social work discourse and practice. Chapter 8 presents a model that pulls together the key themes that underpin the importance of emotions in social work, and also provides a basis for the practical enhancement of this topic moving forward. The preceding section of this chapter concluded with a theoretical and conceptual debate about the efficacy and validity of relationship-based practice. Perhaps the most persuasive and cogent perspective to elicit is that of the individuals who use, access, and experience the services that the social work profession provides. Indeed, the term service user is not without its complexities. Any collective label (however well meaning) can run the risk of reducing the identity of an individual to one who simply uses/consumes/commissions services at the expense of taking a holistic view of them. McLaughlin's (2009) thorough examination of the historical evolution of the terms used to describe people who are in receipt of social work services is highly recommended. For the purposes of the present discussion, however, the crucial message is that these debates are inspired by the importance we place on the relationship between worker and service user, and the key themes of respect, genuineness, and partnership that should permeate them.

Writing from the perspective of a service user contributing to social work qualifying programmes, Dow (2008) emphasizes the importance of his experiences and those of other service users within the content, delivery, and methods of social work education. Dow (2008) and Gee and McPhail (2008) both propose the following conditions as being crucial for the meaningful inclusion of service users' views in social work programmes: no tokenism; genuine shared power; consider the experiences of service users to be at the heart of practice; include service users' voices in decision-making; and clarity of language and communication.

Such service-user involvement in education is increasingly widespread, though requires constant nurturing and enhancement to avoid the routinized and tokenistic tendencies that Dow warns of. The conditions noted above map coherently onto the conditions required of effective relationships in practice. A key aspect of the literature relating to service-user perspectives contains a clear message that people *want to be heard and understood* (Harding and Beresford, 1995; McNeil et al., 2005). This leads us to the quality of the relationships that we develop in social work practice. Put simply, it is through the acknowledgement and exploration of the emotional content of an individual's perspectives that service users can be confident that their uniqueness will be recognized. The alternative approach would be to approach social work relationships in a bureaucratic fashion with the metaphorical checklist and clipboard in hand. If social workers reduce relationships to a functional and procedural process of information-gathering, then, as a consequence, any skills utilized to establish the relationship are simply instrumental.

What is perhaps most striking in the literature reflecting the views of service users over time is that the themes are largely consistent across decades regardless of shifts in paradigms and practices. The following list is drawn from a range of sources (Mayer and Timms, 1970; Harding and Beresford, 1995; McNeil et al., 2005; Ingram, 2013d) and provides an overview of the key and recurrent themes relating to what service users want from social workers who establish a relationship with them:

- To 'hear' and value their perspectives and views.
- To allow service users to define problems and goals – leading to a mutual understanding.
- Social workers should adopt a 'friendly' approach – warmth, empathy, and genuineness.
- Involvement should be purposeful and supportive.
- Social workers should demonstrate respect, honesty, and reliability.
- Social workers should be good listeners.
- They should value uniqueness rather than overly theoretical explanations.

One can see the overlaps with the conditions of a positive relationship proposed by Lishman, highlighted earlier in the chapter (see Figure 4.1). What is crucial is that service users recognize and want social workers to recognize the complexity of their lives and that the route to doing so is via a genuine attempt to build trust and communicate empathy in their relationship.

Howe (2008: 1) suggests that 'emotions define the social work relationship'. The role of emotions is a two-way process in that social workers need to engage with the emotional context of the service user while also recognizing the impact this may have on themselves and in turn their practice. This links with the notion of *sentimental work* proposed by Zapf (2002), which notes the two-way nature of emotional expression and how this can create a dynamic that promotes engagement.

This has recently been echoed and highlighted in the Munro Review of Child Protection. Munro (2011) noted that the relationship between worker and service user is an essential element of 'how' information is gathered, and that to do this effectively the social worker must be able to identify their own emotional responses to the situation and be able to focus the service user's attention on the emotional aspects of their situation. The suggestion is that these elements of practice exist and should be acknowledged and harnessed in conjunction with the focus on procedures and evidence-based practice. This directly builds on the work of Morrison (2007), who highlighted the apparent marginalization of the social work relationship in the face of proceduralist developments and the role that emotional intelligence potentially could have in reclaiming the core skills and processes within the service user–social worker relationship. If we view the importance of the Munro Review (2011) in terms of its significant contribution to national narratives about the direction of social work practice, then it can also be seen in the context of the work on emotional expression by Hochschild (1983) introduced in Chapter 1. It could be argued that social workers are being provided with professional messages about the place of emotions within their practice, and in turn this may contribute to the ways in which emotions are expressed and presented within the practice of social workers. That is, emotions, relationships, and service-users' perspectives are inextricably linked and this is increasingly apparent within key narratives about the social work profession.

Learning activity

- Think of a time when you, as a service user, had a negative interaction with a professional. This could have been with a social worker, teacher, doctor, lawyer, police officer, and so on.
- What was it about the encounter that made it a negative experience?
- Consider the verbal and non-verbal elements of the interaction and how these contributed to your view.
- What were the qualities that were missing in this interaction, and how dependent were you on the approach adopted by the professional?

Empathy: its role within relationship-building

Empathy is a familiar term within social work parlance and is referred to many times throughout this book. It is a term that is readily associated with positive helping relationships; Ingram (2013a) found that almost all the social workers in his study reported empathy to be a key aspect of their practice. It is a key part of a social worker's toolkit and is a desired quality within social work relationships (Lishman, 2009; Hennessey, 2011). The preceding sentence touches on an important aspect of empathy, in that it is both a *skill* and a *quality* that are brought to bear upon and contained within a relationship. Hennessey (2011) notes that the concept is difficult to define, as it can be seen both as a state of mind and individually perceived and experienced. Put simply, it is hard to put into words.

Rogers (1980) suggested that empathy involves an individual tuning into the emotional world of another and being able to communicate this to them. This requires a relationship that moves beyond something that is driven by process but allows space for the conscious and unconscious aspects of an individual's worlds to emerge. Howe (2013) draws parallels with counselling relationships, and the associated need to form trusting and safe relationships to foster the conditions required for empathy. If we consider the messages from service users proposed in the previous section, we can see that it is this type of relationship that is desired by service users with the social workers involved in their lives. Goleman (1985) draws useful parallels between empathy and what we know about positive relationships from attachment theory. Goleman notes that the active identification and response to the feelings of others are the building blocks of secure relationships and in turn can be linked to the foundations of helping relationships.

Hennessey (2011) provides a very helpful set of distinctions between apathy, sympathy, and empathy to shed more light on what we mean by empathy. The starting point is to recognize that the word 'pathy' means 'feeling'. The following points highlight the key distinctions proposed by Hennessey and relate them to the case study:

- *Apathy*: this refers to an absence of feeling. If Molly were to approaches her relationship with Helen in this manner, she would simply disregard and ignore the presence and relevance of Helen's feelings. Indeed, it would be unlikely that an apathetic approach to practice would inspire thinking about emotions associated with the images contained within the photographs in the room. Our knowledge of relationship-building would indicate that this would form a narrow and negative relationship between Molly and Helen.
- *Sympathy*: the addition of the prefix 'sym' introduces the notion that feelings are shared within a relationship and one where there is a relatively unfiltered absorption of the emotions of others. In the case of Molly and Helen, this may manifest itself in Molly feeling very sad about Helen's current circumstances and internalizing the feelings of loss felt by Helen. This does reflect a degree of connection, but it does not allow for exploration of these emotions or a professional distance.
- *Empathy*: this shares the identification of feelings with sympathy, but involves the social worker maintaining a significant degree of self-awareness, so that that deep connection with the service user's feelings is coupled with a clear sense of professional purpose. In our case study, Molly would be able to explore and acknowledge the complex issues of loss experienced by Helen while also placing these issues within the wider context of Helen's life in the residential home. The key strength here is that this emotional connection has a purpose and can lead to a greater sense of understanding/acceptance for Helen and in turn potential ways forward can emerge.

The above suggests that empathy is only really achieved when it feeds back into the relationship. There is little merit in identifying the emotional worlds of others and keeping it to oneself. It only becomes useful if an empathetic approach is adopted where the social worker makes an effort to communicate and share this level of understanding

(Egan, 2010). This involves key social work communication skills such as summarizing, reflecting, and paraphrasing in order for emotions to be named, articulated, and explored. Only through such dialogue can a shared understanding emerge (rather than the intuition of the social worker). This resonates with what Howe (1993: 13) describes as the 'therapeutic sequence' within a psychotherapeutic counselling relationship. This views the wants of service users in relationship with professionals as a process of: 'accept me, understand me, and talk with me'. A central tenet of this approach is the need for the social worker to tune into the narrative of the service user and for this to be underpinned by skills of engagement and the ability to articulate and communicate an understanding and acceptance of the service user's situation.

This is by no means an easy task for social workers, and the pursuit of pure empathy is perhaps an aspiration to strive towards rather than a destination to be reached. As we noted in Chapter 1 and 2, all relationships and associated emotions exist within wider contexts that impact on the way we perceive, articulate, and communicate emotions. If we think about Molly and Helen again, it is likely that Molly's wider caseload will impact upon the time she can allocate to her interactions with Helen. The environment of the residential home may create barriers to relationship-building due to lack of privacy or the power imbalance felt by Helen in terms of the choice she has to engage or not with Molly. Additionally, the degree of empathy within the relationship will be influenced by the quality of the skills deployed by Molly (and indeed Helen) and how this facilitates or impedes a sense of trust and openness. Figure 4.2 illustrates some of the key influences on empathic relationships.

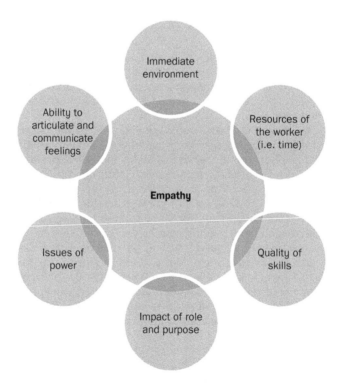

Figure 4.2 Influences on the quality of empathy within social work relationships

The links between empathy and emotional intelligence are self-evident. Salovey and Mayer (1989–90) identify empathy as a key part of their construct of emotional intelligence and link these explicitly to self-awareness and quality of relationships. These links can be made in many areas of social work. For example, the principles of motivational interviewing as an approach to empower service users to address negative behaviours place great emphasis on the need to establish a non-judgemental empathy with service users. This is helpful because it moves relationships away from a disapproving or directive style where the worker and service user occupy polarized positions. Having established a degree of empathy, the service user is encouraged to consider how their behaviour may be impacting on their lives. A key aspect of the approach is that the worker can then encourage the service user to gain an understanding of what would happen if no change were forthcoming. This in turn leads to a sense of self-knowledge and autonomy for the service user when considering the desirability of change.

Emotions, skills, and relationships

The discussion of emotions and social work can sometimes be seen to be a step removed from direct practice. Indeed, this book stresses the need for reflection to unpick the role of emotions. However, the conceptual framework proposed in Chapter 1 underlines how emotions provide us with an almost instantaneous set of signals and signposts to make sense of circumstances and situations that arise in our lives and practice. This highlights the need to remember that emotions have a use and impact in 'real time', and any discussion of the skills that one might utilize in practice must be placed alongside the emotions that will influence and direct them (Ingram, 2013d). For example, given the preceding exploration of empathy, it is clear that the *communication* of empathy will be rooted and expressed through verbal and non-verbal communication. Howe (2013: 124) puts this well when he states: 'Empathy therefore represents a way of being with a client. Every nuance of the other's body language, tone of voice and spoken word is observed and therefore felt. The experience is visceral.' This visceral quality is key here, as it underlines the *inter-personal* aspects of emotions and their communication rather than falling back on the narrow view of emotions being simply *internally* experienced.

There is a body of useful literature focusing on the skills required for effective social work practice (see Thompson, 2002; Koprowska, 2005; Lishman, 2009; Egan, 2010; Woodcock-Ross, 2011). I do not have the space here to address the vast toolkit of skills that social workers draw upon, but it would be useful to pull out what I see as recurrent key themes across the literature and consider their interaction with emotions. I will take these key themes in turn and suggest associated learning tasks to help you contextualize the learning. I will then make links to the case study to further bring the topic to life and consider its application to practice.

Verbal communication

This is the process whereby we communicate through speech. Trevithick (2005) highlights that this is a more complex activity than one might at first believe and notes that one must be conscious of the tone, pitch, speed, and volume of speech. This is relevant when considering the role of emotions and the impact on these elements. For example, it is not uncommon for anxiety to impact on the speed of our vocal delivery. This may have the effect of making us more difficult to understand, and may also communicate the underlying anxiety to whom we are interacting with. This suggests that despite the content and language used within any given scenario, there are also emotional nuances that can impact on the meaning that is conveyed. Another example would be the emphasis on controlling volume and tone within de-escalation techniques for the control of anger (Taylor, 2011). This requires emotional intelligence to acknowledge feelings as they arise, but also underlines the direct links between emotions, skills, and actions.

Learning activity

What feedback have you received from friends, family, service users or colleagues that may have helped you identify the links between your emotions and your verbal communication? If you can't readily think of an example, perhaps you should seek such feedback (i.e. how do people know if you are nervous or under pressure?).

Non-verbal communication

This refers to the ways in which we communicate that do not involve speech. These are often located alongside our verbal communication and interact with it. This interaction may be congruent or contradictory and the role that emotion has within this is central. Examples of non-verbal communication include facial expressions, eye contact, posture, orientation, proximity, and touch (Lishman, 2009). For example, eye contact is a useful way to communicate that one is listening and attending within an interaction. If managed appropriately, it can underline the messages that are being conveyed verbally. However, there is a link between loss of eye contact and nervousness (and even lying). Loss of eye contact is thus likely to transmit these emotions within the interaction and may undermine what one believes to be the explicit verbal message. Another example is the importance of facial expressions and how these interact with the content of our verbal communication. We have already noted the importance placed on warmth by service users, and this may involve smiling to convey this. If social workers don't consider how their emotions can affect their facial expressions, this could have a negative effect on their communication. It is not uncommon for others to enquire if 'something is wrong' when we have not been aware that our emotions are writ large across our face despite our certainty that we have not verbalized them. This underlines the importance of recognizing and developing observational skills to help us to identify the emotional undercurrents within our communication with others.

Learning activity

Take the opportunity to reflect upon your experiences of communicating when highly anxious (i.e. public presentations, important meetings, etc.). Are you aware of any non-verbal habits, tics or tendencies that arise in such circumstances? If possible, it is useful to view video recordings of your performances. This does not need to be in any formal setting and can easily be achieved with any number of mobile devices. Many people dread such analysis and it can indeed be an uncomfortable experience. I suspect this is because it is such a revealing and powerful process, and all the unexpected nuances you observe are simply what everyone else is tuning into when they communicate with you.

Symbolic communication

The previous two aspects of communication are directly associated with our interpersonal skills. Lishman (2009) and Trevithick (2011) highlight that there are less obvious aspects of our approaches and environments that communicate messages about our emotions and thoughts. Regardless of how well we manage the verbal and non-verbal aspects, these may include punctuality, dress, resources, purpose, and the quality of the physical environment. Ferguson (2010) highlights the impacts on our senses arising from the daily environments in which we as social workers practise. The impact of harsh and impoverished environments can have an accumulative effect on the thresholds that social workers hold in terms of their sense of risk and their morale (Ferguson, 2010). This then has a direct impact on the skills and actions we utilize in practice. If we consider the issue of lateness and poor punctuality, it is clear that it can convey a message of disinterest, disorganization, disrespect, and incompetence, all before a social worker has even engaged in the verbal/non-verbal elements of practice. This may be passive and not directly linked to our emotional worlds, or it can be a symptom of the emotions that underpin the rather negative list of messages mentioned above.

Learning activity

Consider the physical environment in which you work (or have worked). Jot down your thoughts about the key features of this environment and consider what messages this may communicate to service users and staff. Do you have any control of this environment? An example might be the quality of the décor of meeting rooms and public spaces.

The ideas explored above provide a platform for identifying a connection between our emotions and the way we engage with service users and others in practice. It lets us see why our self-knowledge is not just about 'why' or 'what' our emotional reactions are but that these will also permeate our communication and how we are perceived, received, and understood within relationships. To ignore the centrality of emotions here would be to detach ourselves from our own practice: something undesirable and unachievable. If we return to the case study, we can place ourselves in the role of a neutral 'fly on the wall' observer and think about how Molly's emotions may interact with her communication. As noted in the case study, Molly has been managing a range of complex emotions, including sadness, identification, and respect. Molly would be keen to focus on her fine communication skills owing to Helen's deteriorating health. For example, Molly might wish to pay particular attention to the qualities (e.g. tone and speed) of her verbal communication to ensure clarity and understanding, but she should also consider how her significant emotional reaction to Helen may affect this. Helen will not simply be tuning into 'what' Molly has to say but how she says it. If Molly's verbal delivery betrays a sense of pity or sadness, this may undermine her ability to engage in a positive and strengths-based manner with Helen. Additionally, Molly might wish to consider her choices in terms of non-verbal communication due to issues relating to Helen's visual impairment. Proximity could be beneficial to enhance Helen's ability to tune into Molly's facial expressions but there is a possibility that Molly's discomfort in the environment of the residential home may move her to subconsciously seek barriers such as tables or beds to manage her feelings. The environment of residential settings is a source of much debate, and issues relating to smell, décor, and quality resources (i.e. food, activities, etc.) will all communicate a sense of the degree of respect and value placed on residents. This will provide a further stream of information within any interaction between Molly and Helen.

Key learning points

- The concept of relationship-based social work has been explored. It was noted that relationships involve an exchange of emotional reactions and these can often be quite complex and difficult to manage. The emphasis is on the uniqueness of each individual's situation and perspectives, and establishing trusting relationships is a foundation for seeking an understanding of these. It was also noted that relationships in social work are inevitably located within the context of professional roles and responsibilities.
- Links were established between the qualities desired of social workers by service users, and the centrality of emotional attunement and relationship-building.
- The concept of empathy was shown to be an active concept involving emotional attunement and communication of this within a relationship.
- The links between emotions and practice skills were established and the presence of emotions in our verbal, non-verbal, and symbolic communication was highlighted. That is, our emotions are communicated through a myriad of ways and our awareness and management of these are crucial in terms of developing a sound skills base.

Further reading

Howe, D. (2013) *Empathy: What it is and why it matters*. London: Palgrave Macmillan.
This is a wide-ranging look at the concept of empathy. It draws from many sources, including psychology, neuroscience, moral philosophy, and counselling skills.

Woodcock-Ross, J. (2011) *Specialist Communication Skills for Social Workers*. London: Palgrave Macmillan.
This accessible and thorough book covers the key aspects of communication in an applied and practical way.

5 | Emotions and written recordings in social work

Chapter objectives

This chapter will:

- Highlight the importance and permanence of writing and the role, status, and purpose of writing in social work.
- Review a broad range of types of writing in social work practice and education and consider the place that emotions may have in the content and process of writing.
- Consider the place of emotions in social work writing in terms of professionalism, transparency, and efficacy.
- Examine the issues and challenges that arise from the proliferation of electronic modes of communication and social media.

An introduction to writing and social work

Writing is a key part of the social work role and task but is often viewed as being onerous and removed from the core business of practice. It would be safe to say that writing reports and case notes is rarely seen as an inspiration to become a social worker: far more likely it is the inter-personal and social justice aspects of the role. This runs the risk, however, of demoting the written articulation of practice to a routinized and procedural task that is simply the recording of what happens in direct practice. This chapter aims to highlight the importance of writing in social work across a range of spheres, including its influence on decision-making, interventions, communication, sharing of information, and accountability. It will also note that the process of writing requires the individual social worker to reflect, edit, prioritize, and present an account of their practice and that this process is subject to differing roles, remits, audiences, proformas, purposes, and functions. The chapter will shed light on the contested place of emotions within writing in social work and will consider the balance between the potential pressure to produce evidence-based accounts (which are characterized by an emphasis on concrete facts and knowledge) and the permissions and ability for social workers to use and record the emotional content of their practice as a stream of information in their written accounts (Ingram, 2013a).

If the task of recording real-life events in writing were simply a facsimile of what happened, then this chapter would have little relevance. Even if we use a filmed recording of an interaction as a 'gold standard' of reproducing what happened, it is immediately evident that the recording means little without the interpretation and retrospective commentary of the participants or the person recording the event. Additionally, the visual recording will not by itself capture the mood, emotions, atmosphere, and wider context of the interaction. Thus, this leads us to a key learning point of this chapter – the inevitable editing and appraisal that will take place when the content of social work practice is subsequently turned into a written account. Hall et al. (2006) suggest it is at this juncture that values, prejudices, purpose, and reflection come into play. Huuskonen and Vakkari (2013) sought the views of social workers on their writing, and noted that the editorial role may be unintentional or a direct response to perceived expectations about content. There are clear links between the conceptual framework of emotions presented in Chapter 1 and this process of appraisal and in turn the developing *meaning* that events have. This allows social workers to prioritize what they view to be the salient issues (in partnership with service users where appropriate), and this will be subject to their own experiences and values as well as prevailing external cultures (i.e. evidence-based practice) (see Figure 5.1).

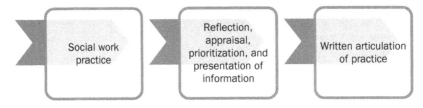

Figure 5.1 From practice to writing

Taylor (2008) highlights the significant influence that writing can have on decision-making forums and the structuring and articulation of practice. Healy and Mulholland (2012) suggest a key aspect of this is the permanent nature of writing. This is clearly much different from speech in the sense that mistakes, indiscretions, and inaccuracies may be corrected, overlooked or simply forgotten within verbal interactions. However, once information is recorded in writing, it attains a status of perceived accuracy (Thompson, 2003) and remains fixed in time. Verbal interactions also occur momentarily and in a specific context. However, written accounts of these interactions can be used and approached by individuals for a range of reasons that are beyond the control of the original author. In the context of social work, this underlines the need for accuracy and a clear sense of purpose in written accounts of practice. O'Rourke (2010) suggests that this can lead to a narrowing of what is perceived to be appropriate content in social work writing, and arguably less tangible elements such as emotions and instincts lose out to the concrete facts. Although accurate and robust information is an essential part of the written articulation of social work, Rustin (2005) notes that crucial information about the realities and experience of some cases may metaphorically be left on the cutting room floor, leading to a lack of depth to the information that can be communicated and shared within and across the professionals involved.

These issues form the basis of this chapter and will be examined in greater detail in conjunction with the following case study. The case study will be presented in two parts to allow for better links to the discussion.

Case study

Derek is a social worker based within an off-campus education project for young people aged 14–16 years who have been excluded from mainstream education. The work of the project is underpinned by a groupwork approach that seeks to equip the young people with social and academic skills and knowledge to support positive transition into work/college. Derek has been working as part of the multi-disciplinary team at the project for the 5 years since he qualified as a social worker.

Derek has been working individually with a young person called Darren to look at his drug use as well as part of a wider group for sports, health, and well-being. Darren is regularly verbally confrontational towards Derek and repeatedly states that he 'is the worst social worker' he has had and that 'he knows nothing about drugs'. Derek does not look forward to his interactions with Darren, and feels undermined and intimidated by Darren's comments. After much reflection, Derek thinks that Darren may have a point in that his knowledge of drug use is limited to policy guidance and literature and he has no clear understanding or proof of the reality of Darren's activities. Derek has also not been receiving supervision due to staff absences, and feels that the quality and efficacy of his practice may be questionable.

Learning activity

- The feelings of intimidation and uncertainty caused by Darren's comments to Derek may require a significant degree of reflection. Why do you think reflection may be important?
- Does the impact of Darren's behaviour towards Derek hold a wider significance in terms of understanding how Darren manages relationships and affects others? How might Derek capture this in a useful way in his case notes and/or reports? What might the challenges and barriers be to this?

Types of writing in social work: the place of emotions

When one talks about writing in social work, it is a rather wide-ranging and disparate umbrella term. This is important, as what is written will be dependent on what we could collectively term the 'four Ws' of writing: What, When, Who, and Why.

- *What* – the content of a piece of writing will vary depending on its purpose. It may have an emphasis on functional information such as dates and names or may require greater depth, drawing upon and analysing information from a range of perspectives to reach defendable recommendations.
- *When* – the timing of committing pen to paper (or whatever method is being used) is crucial in terms of proximity to the event itself, and the potential impact on the lives of service users.
- *Who* – this refers to the audience that the piece of writing is aimed at. This can include courts, professional networks, case conferences, staff teams, agency referral processes, and case file information. The most consistent and pertinent audience for writing in

social work is the subject of the writing itself: the service users and carers. This underlines the importance of clarity, accuracy, and partnership when recording.

- *Why* – whatever writing is undertaken within the role of social worker, it is by definition underpinned by professional roles, codes, and ethics. The reasons behind the requirement to put something into writing are extremely varied, but should always be governed by a clear sense of proportionality, accuracy, and accessibility (Data Protection Act, 1998).

In this section, we will cover three key types of writing in social work, and the 'four Ws' will provide a consistent backdrop to these regardless of the apparent differences. We will look at note-taking, case note records, and report writing. This is certainly not an exhaustive list of the types of writing relating to social work practice, but I have chosen these as they form a familiar chain of writing that links together to produce both a case history and a pivotal information source for interventions and outcomes (see Figure 5.2). While it may appear at first glance a linear process, it will be shown below that writing in social work is a cyclical process where actions and judgements feed into subsequent practice and outcomes. The place that emotions occupy within these types of writing will vary. The role that emotions have within the written articulation of social work is subject to conceptions of professionalism, defensibility, transparency, and culture (Ingram, 2013a).

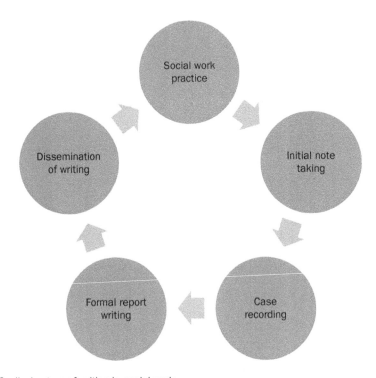

Figure 5.2 Cyclical nature of writing in social work

Taking notes

The act of note-taking is often overlooked as a core aspect of writing in social work. More formal written outputs such as reports are usually held up as the most clearly articulated accounts of practice. What is crucial to remember is that much of what finds its way into more formal pieces of writing often starts life as a scribbled note, doodle or diagram, hastily jotted down either during or soon after an interaction or meeting. The manner in which these notes are taken is often framed within the context of the impact of note-taking on the quality of inter-personal communication (Lishman, 2009). For example, the act of writing may have an impact on a social worker's ability to maintain consistent eye contact within an interaction. The act of writing may also inhibit responses, as service users may become wary about what is being recorded and why. However, a clear benefit of on-the-spot recording is the ability to share and clarify key points of understanding with the service user there and then before any inaccuracies or assumptions may emerge. The overwhelming sense about note-taking is that it is a hugely varied and individual activity, yet provides the very foundations of subsequent written recordings.

Huuskonen and Vakkari (2013) note that at the time of jotting down key points during or following a meeting, the process of editing and prioritizing has begun. Chapter 1 outlined the neurological processes that so swiftly enable us to perceive a stimulus or event and assess its relevance to us. It is this core appraisal and labelling process that results in our attention being drawn to certain pieces of information (whether these be verbal, environmental, personal). In relation to the case study, it is clear that Derek is aware of the negative remarks made to him by Darren. Given his negative emotional response to these comments, it is likely that they will be of significance to him. It may be the case that his emotional response will lead to withdrawal behaviour (Rosenberg, 1990), and even at this early stage Darren's comments may be edited out of the recordings. Alternatively, the emotional response may drive him forwards and encourage him to highlight this verbal aggression as a key issue relating to Darren's situation and relationship skills. Either way, a judgement about relevancy has to be made and this will draw on previous experiences and professional roles and responsibilities.

A final point about note-taking that is of relevance to this discussion is that of timing. In many ways, this is down to personal preference and you will likely have a view about how well you remember events shortly after. From personal experience, I tended to do the bulk of my note-taking sitting in my car following a meeting. This short delay of a few minutes meant that I had to review my memories of what happened and I would naturally be drawn to information that seemed most interesting to me or was most memorable. This draws us back to the chapter on reflection and the need for social workers to consider not just what seems important to them, but *why*. As soon as we begin to enter a reflective process (even a rather crude one like thinking back to a meeting that one has just left), we begin to draw on emotions, values, and experiences. As noted in Chapter 1, these are what help us make sense of the world around us. But, as we move onto more formalized writing, we may find that our presence as the narrator/author becomes less clear.

Case notes: accounting for social work

The maintenance of case notes or case records is a key aspect of social work practice and provides social workers with an opportunity to produce detailed written accounts of the content of their practice. These case notes will contain a range of different types of information that, when brought together, help to form a history and evolving narrative of practice. Case notes need to contain the sort of information that would be useful, indeed essential, for anyone who required a clear sense of the content of that particular case. This brings us back to the importance of considering the 'audience', and for case notes this includes you (the author), service users, agency colleagues, line managers, associated professional groups, and the courts. This potentially wide-ranging readership means that you will need to tailor your writing so that is useful and accessible. The Data Protection Act (1998) makes clear the need for case notes to be accurate, relevant, proportional, and up to date.

Healy and Mulholland (2012) state that case notes should be factual and based on concrete evidence. This sort of information may involve names, addresses, dates, times, and verifiable events. It is clear from this interpretation of case notes that the emotional elements of practice (both in terms of the social worker's emotions and those of the service user) may have a rather vulnerable status. Healy and Mulholland go on to note that where 'opinion' is offered (i.e. something less concrete and tangible), it must be explicitly labelled as such so the reader can assess its efficacy and relevancy. While it is hard to argue with the principles noted above, it is important that we consider the messages that this sends to social workers about the type of information that is permissible in their writing of practice and the impact this has on the representation of emotions in case-note writing.

Voices of practitioners: Grace, a children and families social worker

'I do accept that I have emotions in regard to my work, but when putting them into my written assessments or explaining them to clients/parents, I feel I can muddle the situation.'

Grace highlights the notion that emotions can 'muddle' the clarity of written aspects of practice. Indeed, she suggests that is also difficult to share and explain emotional aspects of her practice with service users. This brings into question the impact this might have on transparency and genuineness. This highlights the direction that the 'editing' process might take when concrete evidence and facts are seen as the gold standard.

A great deal of artistry is required to capture the less concrete aspects of social work practice (England, 1986). Indeed, it is essential that we are able to articulate and co-produce accounts of the thoughts and perspectives of service users. These may not be 'certain' but, if left unrecorded, are simply not available to influence subsequent use of the case records. Munro (2011) highlights the importance of social workers' emotional reactions and their important role as a stream of information when making assessments. If we consider the editing that takes place at the initial note-taking stage, we can begin to see how a further layer of selectivity takes place when turning these notes into formal case note recordings.

Taylor (2008) proposes a further dimension for social workers to consider when they approach the task of presenting their practice in writing – the role of language. Taylor took an ethno-methodological approach to social work reports, focusing on *how* information is presented and in turn the impact this has on the message that is transmitted. Roose et al. (2009) highlight that it is often in the words we choose that emotions and motivations begin to surface. For example, Derek might write: 'as expected, the house was full of friends and associates and Darren's mother refused to let them leave'. The most basic reading of this would be that the house was busy and Darren's mother wanted everyone to remain in the house for the meeting. However, if we highlight the phrase 'as expected', we begin to sense some pre-judgement and a sense of irritation creeping into the narrative (my use of the word 'creeping' here is equally evocative of my views). The use of the word 'associates' underlines a sense of lack of clarity about the status of the people in the house, and the choice of the word 'refused' is very powerful and suggests that Derek appraised her motives as being confrontational and inflexible. Thus, the key message is that even what appears to be a detached reporting of events, can have an emotional content seen within the words used.

In relation to the case study, Derek may feel comfortable noting down the concrete aspects of the case such as Darren's attendance record, the groups in which he participates, and the visible outcomes of the project's work such as test results and achievements. These parts of the narrative can be evidenced and will likely be part of a shared view with Darren. The less clear aspects of the case, such as suspicions of Darren's drug, use will be less easy to put into writing, especially as Derek is experiencing a degree of anxiety relating to Darren's treatment of him. This is where the need for clarity of information comes into play. If we accept that case notes should contain all the salient aspects of a case, then it could be argued that it is crucial this information is recorded at this point in the process. Healy and Mulholland (2012) note that the contents of case notes can be co-produced with service users, and that reflection on the impact of behaviours can provide a powerful source of information for both parties. Taylor (2008) stresses that whatever the content of written recordings in social work, it is at best a selective account. This should provide you with some confidence to include and own the less certain or troubling aspects of a case. It would be very useful potentially for Derek (and Darren) to record the concerns about the way Darren speaks about drug use. Indeed, the process of writing may provide Derek with a springboard to explore these issues with Darren, which otherwise may have been marginalized. The crucial step that social workers must take when writing case notes is to reveal themselves as narrator and curator of the recorded information (Taylor, 2008). By doing so, any concerns about the transparency or validity of case notes can be navigated.

Report writing: pulling the written information together

There are a myriad of social work reports with a similarly diverse range of purposes and functions. What is common to all of these is that reports require social workers to provide a clear and focused account of the case, an assessment of all the available information, an evaluation of progress, and recommendations for subsequent action and decision-making. It is through such reports that decisions are made and information is communicated across a range of professional networks and stakeholders. That is, formal social work reports are the most explicit and externally consumed written accounts of practice. The content of these reports aims to achieve the most appropriate and relevant outcomes for service users and needs to locate the service user within their social environment (Thompson, 1998). As indicated earlier in this chapter, report writing forms part of a writing process and the quality of the information contained in reports will in part be reliant on the quality of previous written records.

The important role that social reports can have in the decision-making process strengthens the need for accuracy and clarity. The place of concrete factual knowledge is important here, and the need to clearly articulate the sources and reliability of streams of information is paramount. Healy and Mulholland (2012) note that good report writing should highlight why certain facts are deemed to be salient and what criteria were applied to guide this process. This is very interesting for our discussion if we consider that there is by definition an editorial role from the very moment pen is applied to paper.

If we are to write reports that are transparent and make clear why certain issues are highlighted, there is a need to record decisions and include certain types of information at earlier stages.

The second part of the case study will help us explore some of these issues relating to report writing more fully.

Case study

Derek has become increasingly concerned about Darren's physical appearance at the project: he is regularly pale, unclean, and 'spaced out'. This prompted Derek to undertake a home visit to explore what might be happening to Darren outside of the project. Derek was immediately struck by the significant number of visitors to the house and was unhappy about being asked to wait outside the living room for a few minutes while several people could be heard moving items around the room and laughing. The explanation given was that they were 'tidying up'. Derek was unsettled by the darkness in the room and could clearly smell marijuana smoke. Due to the number of people in the room and the insistence of Darren's mother that they remain, Derek felt it inappropriate to discuss Darren's situation and said he would make arrangements to come back at a more convenient time.

Later that day, Derek is asked to write an update report for a case review hearing. He is conscious that Darren hopes to be relieved of his supervision order and the issue of his drug use is central to this decision. Derek is also aware that Darren's family social worker intends to report that Darren no longer uses drugs of any kind and is making great progress. The timescale for this report is short, so Derek will need to base it on the information available to him.

Learning activity

- To what extent do you record observations and associated emotional reactions in your written recordings? Would they form part of your case notes?
- What might be the risks of omitting these uncertain aspects of a case from written recordings?

This additional development in the case of Darren poses many challenges for Derek. It highlights the role that pressures of time can have on the process of writing in social work practice. The home visit has raised more concerns for Derek regarding potential drug use within Darren's home environment, and the difficulty of communicating with Darren's mother to explore any concerns he may have. Derek will need to consider the impact of his emotional reaction to Darren when deciding whether to prioritize this new information, as he may need to consider whether he is interpreting the events in the home through the lens of his 'gut feeling' about Darren's situation. Given the previous points made about the desirability for verifiable facts in reports, Derek may find it uncomfortable to include the as yet unclear aspects of the case. There will also be pressure from Darren to provide a positive report of his progress (in line with others involved) to enable him to have his supervision order lifted. To counterbalance this, Derek is required to provide an up-to-date, honest, and holistic account of his work with Darren.

Voices of practitioners: Robin, a children and families social worker

'The greatest resource you have is yourself – and creativeness and being able to form relationships with service users and other services, always trying to get the best result and be positive . . . your emotion and you do have a gut feeling and maybe do a police check to check it out and that is professional, but that emotion is not included in reports and case notes.'

Derek provides a persuasive case for the role of emotions within his practice and provides a lucid example of how a gut feeling may move you to undertake an action such as a 'police check', but that the driver (in this case, the gut feeling) is not considered appropriate to record. This may lead to an unclear and incomplete account of how and why particular decisions were made.

One way of untangling the tensions about what constitutes appropriate information in reports, and how the emotional content of practice is recorded or edited out, is to access key messages within professional codes of practice (NISSC, 2004; SSSC, 2009; BASW, 2012b). Healy and Mulholland (2012) state that case notes are focused and factual accounts of the process and ongoing assessment of practice, which can be used as an historical record by the individual social worker, colleagues and, potentially, service users (hence the new developments in the case of Darren may have a place here). The same authors note that formal reports have a direct impact on decision-making forums and processes, and as such need to be accurate, fair, and clear. What unites these two types of writing and any other written recordings in social work is that they are underpinned by the codes of practice in terms of their content and focus. For example, they should seek to acknowledge and value the views and perspectives of service users. Taking this link to professional codes and values a step further, Ingram (2013a) found that social workers viewed a perceived emphasis on 'facts' as an obstacle and deterrent in terms of writing about emotions and uncertainties in reports. It seemed that accuracy and validity were linked to process outcomes and tangible certainties. If we consider the discussion earlier in this chapter about the importance and inescapability of unknowns and uncertainty in practice, then to remove and edit the emotional aspects of practice from written recording would result in a less than 'accurate' or 'factual' account. This could turn the view of emotions and writing on its head, in the sense that we could argue that to write an account of practice that is authentic and seeks to present the process and content of practice in an open and genuine fashion *must* involve discussion of emotions and the relationship between worker and service user (Munro, 2011). Given the conceptual framework of emotions that underpins this book, it is clear that emotions are an important part of the way social workers perceive, think, and act within their practice. If we accept that it is important for social workers to engage in reflection about the sources of their emotions, then it is questionable whether it is authentic for these thoughts and actions to be edited out of their accounts of practice.

Taylor (2008) provides the vivid metaphor of 'show and tell' to help guide the thinking of social workers writing reports. The familiar school activity of asking young children to stand up in front of their class and discuss an object with their classmates, providing both a visual 'prop' and an explanatory narrative alongside it, fits well with the balance between concrete facts and broader discussion within reports.

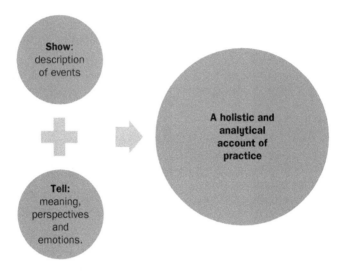

Figure 5.3 Show and tell in written accounts of social work

Figure 5.3 highlights that the simple presentation of explicitly known and provable facts in the tradition of scientific writing is akin to standing in front of your class holding your object up for scrutiny with little description of 'what' it means to you or 'why' it is important. The 'telling' part adds the depth. It allows you to note why something is important to you. It opens the door to different perspectives and feelings, and encourages the audience to consider what is important and relevant to them. This maps well on to the role of report writing, and chimes with the need for social workers to have confidence in presenting and using their judgements and emotional responses (Munro, 2011). If we link this back to Derek's dilemma, we can see that there is an opportunity for him to write a report that draws on known and established facts alongside the more fluid and blurry perspectives of the many voices involved as well as emerging themes and issues that have yet to be fully examined or understood. This process is by definition an emotional one, which requires the appraisal of events, the application of meaning to them, and a presentation of them within the prevailing culture and context. Clearly, there is a role for supervision here and the rehearsal and exploration of complexities of practice could usefully be addressed in that forum. But Derek is not receiving regular supervision, and as Ferguson (2005) suggests, this can lead to a suppression of the difficult and uncomfortable aspects of practice.

Reflective writing: creating space to think about emotions

The preceding discussion about the challenges of locating the emotional content of practice in formal recording and report writing emphasizes the need to consider who the audience for the writing is and what purpose it is to serve. This understandably raises the bar in terms of a need for clarity, accuracy, and communicability. Social workers may also be able to examine their practice in greater detail in a forum one step removed from the formal recordings contained within case files – namely, reflective writing. In Chapter 3, we examined the place of emotions within the context of reflective practice and the central role that this plays in allowing social workers to understand their use of self and explore the conscious and unconscious factors at play in their inter- and intra-personal worlds. Given what we now know about the selectivity involved in the process of prioritizing information when writing, it is even more relevant to consider how we can shine a light on what contributes to those decisions.

Ward (2010) highlights the potential role that reflective writing can have in enhancing an understanding of one's practice and of one's self in relation to it. The Social Work Task Force (DCSF, 2009) suggests that the inter- *and* intra-personal qualities of social workers are important, and that opportunities for reflection and space to develop these qualities are crucial. The use of reflective writing would seem to be a useful forum for such activities. Ingram (2013a), however, found that qualified social workers reported that they had little or no opportunity or expectation to write reflectively. The pressures of time and lack of an audience for such writing were cited as factors. Ward (2010) and Moon (2004) suggest that an audience is not required for reflective writing to be useful. It is the process of ordering, editing, and thinking associated with reflective writing that is key. This is in line with the suggestion of Hafford-Letchfield (2009) that learning cultures within social work organizations can be informal and *self-led* as well as more formally structured.

From the perspective of a lecturer on an undergraduate social work programme, I am struck by the disconnection between the content and messages within our programme (and programmes across the country) in terms of the importance of reflective writing and the apparent lack or inconsistency of it in practice. On our undergraduate programme, students are required to write reflective accounts during and at the end of all practice learning opportunities and prepare for supervision sessions by maintaining a reflective journal. The reason that students are required to do this is the belief that it is important for students to think about their practice in a critical and analytical way and record this accordingly. We encourage them to consider their emotional reactions alongside identifying other sources that impact what they do and why they do it. Through this process, students are able to demonstrate a deeper understanding of their practice and their development as a social worker. This links well to the conceptual framework proposed in Chapter 1, as it mirrors the reflexive element of emotional appraisal (Schachter and Singer, 1962; Rosenberg, 1990) and the meanings we are then able to attach to our emotional responses. Ward (2010) notes how important it is for education and practice to have strong links and synergies, and this seems to be a clear example of where the pressures of resources and time, when coupled with an outcomes-focused conception of supervision and practice, drive a wedge between the two.

It would be hard to argue against the usefulness of reflection and its written form, yet it appears to be marginalized due to competing pressures and approaches. Hennessey (2011) and Howe (2008) both note the importance of being able to step away from one's practice and have space to express and explore the complex and confusing elements of that practice. Whether this is undertaken in writing or within other forums such as supervision, it is clear that a cultural ethos needs to be developed that encourages and values it. If such a cultural shift is made, then a context of trust and safety may be developed to support it. Beddoe (2010) emphasizes that trust is essential if the uncertainties and complexities of the practice can be revealed and explored. Howe (2008) notes that such a culture mirrors that of the desirable conditions of a relationship between worker and service user.

The scope of this chapter does not allow for a full coverage of reflective writing techniques but see Moon (1999) listed in the further reading at the end of this chapter. A very pertinent approach to reflective writing, however, is that of critical incident analysis (Tripp, 1993; Davies and Kinloch, 2000). It fits really well with the conceptual framework of emotions that underpins this book, as it is premised on the individual social worker identifying an event that they appraise to be of significance. A critical incident does not have to be a dramatic event, but one that becomes more complex once unpicked and examined (Tripp, 1993). Davies and Kinloch (2000) suggest that often it is the emergence of a question from oneself or another that prompts the need for deeper reflection. In the case of Derek, it may be a colleague asking him if he is worried about Darren. This may prompt Derek to identify his home visit to Darren's house as a critical incident and one worth unpacking.

An excellent resource relating to the use of critical incident analysis is Crisp et al. (2005), listed in the further reading at the end of this chapter. The suggestions below draw on this work and that of Parker et al. (1995) and Davies and Kinloch (2000).

Learning activity

Identify a practice situation or event that was significant to you.

- Write a brief account of the event in order to set the scene – who, where, and why.
- What was your role as you understand it and what knowledge underpinned this role?
- Record your emotional responses at the time of the event and why you think you experienced these.
- How do you think the other people involved may have felt at that time? Did they tell you? Did you share how you felt?
- Thinking back to the event now, what are your emotional responses to it? How have these impacted your thinking and decision-making? What have you learnt about yourself and how can this be used to achieve positive outcomes?
- How might this experience provide a foundation for future practice and your responses within in it?
- What are the key learning needs that arise out of this?

This process has been adapted to place greater emphasis on use of self and emotions. It could easily be adjusted to shine a light on other aspects of practice such as organizational culture or the role of theory. The use of critical incident analysis is well established in social work education but is less evident within qualified practice. There are likely to be issues of time and resources at play (Crisp et al., 2005), as well as the feeling that this learning is less important once qualified. The latter scenario would be rather concerning given the dangers inherent in routinized practice, which sidesteps consideration of the emotional and inter-personal aspects of social work (Ferguson, 2005; Ward, 2010).

In the case of Derek, we can hypothesize about the potential benefits of engaging in written reflection of this kind. The initial scene-setting aspect of the process is useful because it will help Derek clarify the purpose of the visit and also consider the impact of the environment and those present. Addressing his emotional responses may well provide unexpected results, in that Derek may note feelings of fear relating to the adults present coupled with a surprising sense of satisfaction that the possible drug use in the house confirms his suspicions. Going deeper, Derek must then consider *why* he felt this way. It may be that his fears about the dark crowded room are linked to previous experiences of being physically threatened in the past. He may also begin to realize that he is selectively seeking information that confirms his suspicions (Collins and Daley, 2011). The prompt to consider the feelings and actions of others is potentially very important. Darren's mother may wish for her friends to stay to provide support and/or out of fear of the professional role and remit of the social work department. That is, her behaviour might have been an attempt to re-balance perceived power differentials. This may allow Derek to reframe his view of the situation, or at the least provide him with alternative perspectives to consider and in so doing lay some foundations for discussions with Darren's mother in the future. It will also prompt him to think about why he chose to end the home visit when he did. The initial justification was linked to confidentiality, but perhaps deeper reflection would reveal a desire to extricate himself from the situation and avoid asking difficult questions about Darren's possible drug use. These reflections (among others) will then provide Derek with a deeper sense of his emotional responses and the origins of them. Perhaps most importantly, however, this self-knowledge will then contribute to his understanding of the significance of his relationship with Darren and his family and the need to consider issues of power (from all perspectives).

There will of course be an effect on the more formal writing arenas, with Derek better equipped to articulate the sources of his judgements and the reasons that underpin his subsequent decision-making. Roose et al. (2009) highlight a participative approach to report writing that reduces the potential power imbalances by encouraging that genuine value be placed on the perspectives (congruent or otherwise) of service users and social workers within reports. In this case, Derek's reflection provides him with a potential in-road to explore the views of Darren's mother.

It is important to note that reflective writing is as much at the mercy of subjectivities, bias, selectivity, and avoidance as any other form of writing (Taylor, 2003). Indeed, it is because of those messy aspects of practice that uncomfortable dilemmas and conflicts emerge. As noted above, there needs to be a sense of safety and space for unresolved uncertainties and weaknesses to be addressed. Where that sense of safety is absent, there is a possibility that you may simply massage your reflections by selecting issues that do not reveal aspects of yourself that could prove challenging or complex. One solution of course is to engage in self-reflection to circumvent this issue; otherwise, organizational culture and supervision could address such aspects of reflection and practice. These issues will be picked up later in this book.

Writing and social work in the digital age

Much of what we have discussed in this chapter refers to written tasks and activities, which, at least metaphorically, involve putting pen to paper. The permanence and power of the written word have been examined and we have noted the need for accuracy, clarity, and brevity when recording information about social work practice. The rapid rise of digital media and social networking provides social work with many new opportunities and challenges (BASW, 2012a), thus adding another layer of complexity to writing related to social work. It is likely that the majority of readers of this book will be regularly engaged with writing in digital formats, whether it be on a personal basis (emails, social media, etc.) or a professional basis (electronic recording systems, emails, web-based resources, etc.). Reamer (2006) notes that this creates a rather permeable boundary between the personal and professional spheres and requires social workers to have the skill, knowledge, and ethical guidance to navigate such terrain.

Watling and Rogers (2012) provide a thorough examination of the knowledge and skills required of social workers in a digital society. In terms of the place that emotions inhabit within this sphere, several important issues need to be considered. The interface between the personal and professional spheres has been at the heart of our discussion of emotions in terms of emotional intelligence and the need for social workers to consider their emotional expression within their professional roles. The most striking aspect of social media and social work is that writing that is intended to be read within a personal or private arena can be readily accessed and/or shared within a much more public arena. This is important if one considers the stages of reflection and self-knowledge acquisition required of social workers to help them manage and understand their emotional responses. The immediacy of online opportunities for writing can circumvent such opportunities and can lead to unguarded written comments about practice and the emotions associated with it.

This personal/professional boundary is made all the more relevant when we consider the need for social workers to adhere to professional codes of practice across all public spheres of their lives (BASW, 2012b), and issues of privacy, respect, confidentiality, and consent all potentially come into play when social workers write on digital platforms. This has not been lost on regulatory bodies, and policy and guidance have been forthcoming to help social workers address these issues (SSSC, 2011; BASW, 2012b). While such guidance points to potential opportunities for good practice, the key unifying element is a cautionary tone emphasizing that social workers will be traceable and accountable as the 'authors' of any online written activity. This links directly with the issue of professional boundaries and suggests that social workers must adopt a sense of *e-professionalism*, whereby all online activities take cognizance of professional responsibilities (Megele, 2012). In the case of Derek, he may wish to share a generalized and anonymized (I am taking this part for granted) sense of his frustrations at work with a close friend via social media. While on one level this may appear to be a private act, it runs the risk of becoming a publicly visible presentation of emotion and practice that could have a significant negative impact on his professional credibility and relationships. It is useful at this point to link back to the importance of social context and emotions as discussed in Chapter 1 (Turner and Stets, 2005). The digital sphere provides social workers with a moving target when trying to tune into the prevailing culture in terms of emotional expression. What seems like an informal and private culture of unguarded openness and emotional exploration can quickly cross over into a public professional representation of a situation.

Learning activity

- List the various forms of social media and digital communication that you use, read, and access on a regular basis.
- Are you aware of the availability/privacy of such communications? Can you identify potential challenges for you in terms of maintaining personal/professional boundaries?

The use of electronic means of communication is of course not only experienced at this difficult personal/professional boundary. Perron et al. (2010) note that relationships increasingly have both an *online* and *offline* aspect to them. This can be illustrated by the proliferation of online support groups and networks that social workers can contribute to and/or link service users to. Indeed, the knowledge of web-based resources is increasingly part of the social worker's toolkit (Watling and Rogers, 2012). Reamer (2006) notes that an emphasis on the role of online communication in terms of relationships means that emails and texts messages are a cogent method of communication within a professional relationship. However, he warns that due to the aforementioned blurring of personal/professional boundaries, the professional purpose of such communications must be clear to both parties. Thus, electronic communication can help build relationships and lead to positive outcomes for service users, but the underpinning professional codes and ethics of social work must be followed at all times.

Key learning points

- The process of writing in social work is subject to the priorities, emotions, experiences, and context of the social worker.
- Perceptions of professional role and purpose will impact on the place that fluid variables such as emotional reactions have within the written articulation of practice.
- The inclusion of emotions and the uncertainties of practice produce a richer and more authentic account of practice and in turn may further support subsequent decisions and actions.

Further reading

Crisp, B.R., Green Lister, P. and Dutton, K. (2005) *Integrated Assessment: New assessment methods. Evaluation of an innovative method of assessment: critical incident analysis*. Working Paper. Glasgow: Scottish Institute for Excellence in Social Work Education [http://www.iriss.org.uk/sites/default/files/sieswe-nam-evaluation-critical-incident-analysis-2005-02.pdf].
This paper provides many tools and examples to help social workers to begin to unpick the complexities of their practice and develop ways of recording them in writing.

Moon, J. (1999) *Reflection in Learning and Professional Development*. London: RoutledgeFalmer.
A very readable book that has many practical tips for writing and reflective practice.

Watling, S. and Rogers, J. (2012) *Social Work in a Digital Society*. London: Learning Matters.
This book covers the impact of 'the digital society' on social work and provides advice, guidance, and practical tools to help social workers make sense of this constantly evolving landscape.

6 | Emotions, supervision, and support

Chapter objectives

This chapter will:

- Consider the opportunities for social work supervision to provide a forum for exploring the emotional content of practice.
- Examine a range of conceptualizations of the supervisory relationship within social work practice and education, and highlight the challenges associated with these in terms of exploring and reflecting upon emotions.
- Highlight other sources of support and guidance, including group supervision, peer supervision, informal peer support, and out-sourced supervision.
- Locate the discussion within the context of current social work policy and narratives, and provide suggestions for the conditions and approaches that may facilitate and safeguard the place of emotions within supervision.

Emotions and supervision: setting the scene

This book has made regular reference to the need for social workers to have opportunities to reflect and think about their practice. In doing so, it is hoped that social workers will be able to take a step back from the 'doing' of their practice and begin to examine more closely the emotions, values, context, and knowledge at play. This is not new to social work and there is a strong tradition of providing formal and regular supervision to social workers to help support them to be effective, accountable, and supported in their roles. The preceding two sentences contain some crucial cornerstones of supervision that are pertinent when considering the place of emotions within supervision and when thinking about the function of supervision more widely.

Many models of supervision have been presented over the years, highlighting a range of emphases and functions. For the purposes of this chapter, I use the classic model proposed by Kadushin (1985) as a starting point. Kadushin suggested that supervision has *managerial*, *supportive*, and *educational* functions. The first thing to note about this is that supervision is multi-functional and that these functions may vary in their compatibility and relevance. Ferguson (2005) notes that the ability for supervisory relationships to allow space for social workers to reflect upon their experiences is negatively impacted upon by external factors such as heavy caseloads and an emphasis on managerial approaches to supervision. As a reader of this book, you will have your own context to consider and at times the balance of the aforementioned functions will fluctuate.

This chapter will allow you to consider the opportunities and challenges involved in formal supervision and the importance of relationships and partnership working within it. Alternative sources of support and guidance will be examined to help you consider the breadth and depth of opportunities that you may seek in differing practice contexts. The following case study will be referred to throughout the chapter to help you make links between the discussion and your own experiences – past, present or future.

Case study

Simon has recently been promoted to a senior social work role within a busy children and families team. As part of his new duties, he is to provide supervision to several colleagues. This is a new experience for Simon and he has undertaken a half-day training course that introduced him to the paperwork involved and the expectations regarding frequency of sessions. Simon has had many supervisors over the years and has had some positive experiences in which he felt well supported and understood, and others where he felt rather vulnerable and undervalued. Simon has not worked in this team previously and does not yet have a sense of the way supervision is delivered by others. In addition to this new role, Simon is an active practice educator, and is currently providing supervision to a social work student from the local university who is currently undertaking a practice learning opportunity within the team.

One of Simon's new supervisees is Ela. She has been working in the team for 4 years and has been very quiet and guarded in supervision. She has hinted at struggling with the size and intensity of her caseload but when Simon tries to explore her work with her, she appears defensive and provides only a functional description of her activities. The student Simon practice educates is called Elizabeth. She is in her final year and comes across as enthusiastic and competent. Due to the stage she is at on her social work programme, she is carrying a significant caseload and is expected to operate with a degree of autonomy while using supervision as a forum to reflect and receive guidance. Elizabeth will qualify and graduate if she passes the practice learning opportunity. The university course provides information and direction about what is expected in terms of the depth of reflection and analysis required within supervision.

Learning activity

- From your experience, consider how the paperwork associated with supervision structures the focus and content. Does this facilitate discussions about the emotional content of practice?
- What might the inhibitors and facilitators be for exploring the emotions for Ela and Elizabeth? Do these differ for a qualified practitioner and a student? If so, why?
- List the skills and qualities that Simon should possess to create a safe and engaging environment for supervision. Create a list of the opposite of these qualities and skills. Reflect upon your experiences and compare these two lists against your supervisory experiences.

Exploring the functions of supervision

Education and developmental functions

The educational aspect of this model points clearly to supervision being a forum in which workers learn and develop personally and professionally. Hawkins and Shohet (2006) note this developmental function and suggest that it is underpinned by opportunities to reflect on all aspects of practice and the knowledge that may underpin this. This reflective process will involve the identification of the individual worker's emotions, values, and motivations in relation to the decisions and actions taken in practice. A typical discussion may address the following areas:

- Description of content of practice.
- Why particular decisions were made. What were the alternatives?
- What sources of knowledge, theory, policy, and legislation might underpin this?
- What was the emotional content of this interaction? How might others involved view this?
- How does this fusion of self-knowledge and wider knowledge help the supervisee understand their practice and in turn inform future practice?

This learning-centred approach to supervision is intended to allow social workers to take a step back and think about their actions and decisions (Noble and Irwin, 2009). Beddoe (2010) notes that some degree of reflection and learning is essential to avoid practice becoming routinized. The professional experience that supervisors do/should possess comes into play here, as the various parts of practice are examined, discussed, and understood in partnership. What is particularly crucial in terms of the focus of this book is that this learning is about a combination of 'hard' streams of knowledge such as theory and legislation and also 'soft' streams of knowledge such as emotions and values (Ingram et al., 2014). This allows for emotions to be seen *as a part of practice* that can help explain, motivate, and direct practice rather than be purely contained in the supportive function of supervision. This model of supervision is of course at the core of social work education supervisory relationships. I suspect this is because it is fundamentally understood that students are engaged in learning. To suggest that qualified workers are not (or at least less) required to learn or develop through supervision overlooks the importance of the Professional Capabilities Framework (PCF; College of Social Work, 2012), such as ongoing professional learning, reflection, and accountability.

If we consider the conceptual framework of emotion presented in Chapter 1, it is clear that each individual experience we encounter as social workers will be subject to an intricate and ever-changing set of inter-personal, intra-personal, conscious, subconscious, and socially constructed emotional markers. This further underlines the need for a supervisory arrangement that allows for reflection and learning. In relation to the case study, it is evident that Simon needs to consider the educational function of his supervisory relationships. In relation to his practice learning supervision with Elizabeth, this will in part be supported by the academic requirements of her social work programme and the need to evidence links between theory and practice alongside an ability to engage in and articulate reflective practice. This will be underpinned and motivated by academic requirements to complete written work such as reflective diaries, critical incident analyses, and practice portfolios (Lomax et al., 2010). This is perhaps less clear in relation to Ela, who feels less able to share the full complexity of her workload despite a strong sense that she would benefit greatly from it. Simon could help Ela to identify the emotional content of her practice as a core aspect of it, rather than something she feels needs to be edited or suppressed. Although (as we shall see later in this chapter) it would be very helpful for Ela to be included in co-producing the focus and content of supervision, it is likely that Simon will need to identify how to introduce and safeguard the educational function of supervision from the outset of the supervisory relationship. Both Simon and Ela will be able to point to national guidance that reinforces and supports the need for an educative function in supervision, and guidance such as the Continuous Learning Framework (SSSC, 2008) and the PCF (College of Social Work, 2012).

Supportive function of supervision

This aspect of the supervisory relationship might at first glance seem the most comfortable home for the discussion of the emotional elements of practice. This would be the case if we narrowed our conception of emotions down to those relating to resilience and coping. While these are essential, our conceptual framework of emotions requires us to consider the pervasive presence of emotions across all aspects of practice relationships, decisions, and actions. That said, Hawkins and Shohet (2006) rightfully emphasize the profound emotional impact that social work practice can have on individual workers and in turn their functioning. Hennessey (2011) vividly notes that social workers are the key resource in social work practice and as such need to be nurtured to continue to function well. Collins (2007) echoes this and suggests that the ability to share and explore the emotional content of practice can foster resilience and ameliorate stress. This suggests that it goes beyond simply being 'a problem shared', to a process in which new strategies and coping mechanisms can evolve. Collins (2007) provides a welcome balance to this discussion by noting that the emotional responses of social workers to practice are not restricted to difficult and negative emotions such as fear, anxiety, and anger. They are also characterized by joy, satisfaction, and enthusiasm, which, if given a forum to be aired and examined, can lead to a nourishing and replenishing function of supervision. In many ways, the most important aspect of this process is that there is *throughput into ongoing practice* and this is only possible where emotional responses (of whatever nature or hue) are permitted and validated.

Agass (2002) suggests that given the fluid and complex nature of social work practice, supervision should provide a forum in which social workers' emotions can be contained. This is echoed by Cornish (2011), who speaks of the concept of *negative capability*. In simple terms, this refers to the ability of workers to function while being uncertain about the content or meaning of their practice. This scenario will be familiar to anyone who has experience of social work practice, in that the focus, direction, and information available in any given situation are fluid and ever-changing. This uncertainty may be characterized by anxiety, and the supervisory relationship can provide a forum in which such uncertainties are contained to allow for further thought and reflection. Hawkins and Shohet (2006) argue that the personal and professional spheres of the social worker are inextricably intertwined. Ingram (2013c) found that for some social workers, this aspect of supervision was not immediately apparent, and to reveal uncertainties might risk a negative judgement about competence or health and well-being. For the emotional aspects of social work to be shared within supervision, there needs to be explicit permission to do so. This must be underpinned by a willingness and awareness that emotional confusion, anxiety, and/or satisfaction are fluid states. This is very important, as it allows space for the supportive function to be ongoing rather than rushing to a snap judgement about emotions and practice.

Simon will likely find it challenging to convey the supportive elements of supervision to Ela and Elizabeth. This is not because of any hypothetical assertions about Simon's willingness or ability to engage in a supportive manner, but that this process is by definition two-way in nature and requires trust and a lowering of (possibly natural) defences on the part of the supervisees. Simon's task is to communicate that there is space and safety to explore the challenges and complexities of practice. Although the two supervisory contexts differ, what unites them is the potential perception that the management/ assessment aspects threaten and undermine the freedom to explore difficulties and uncertainties. This is hardly surprising given the attractiveness of appearing knowledgeable, certain, and professional within both contexts. The answer to this conundrum will emerge throughout this chapter, but at this juncture it is worth noting that Simon will be required to utilize the skills of relationship-building and emotional intelligence to establish relationships that tune into the emotional worlds of his supervisees but must do so in a way that also communicates to them that they are heard and valued (Ingram, 2013d).

Managerial and quality assurance functions of supervision

If the previous supportive element of supervision seemed the best fit for the emotional content of social work practice, then the managerial function of supervision may appear to be the most challenging and adversarial. Payne (2000) notes that it is within this function that the standards and quality of practice are monitored and upheld. Hawkins and Shohet (2006) identify the positive facets of this aspect of supervision, in the way it fits very comfortably with maintaining ethical practice and positive outcomes for service users. It may also be reassuring for social workers to have their practice placed clearly within a wider organizational, professional, and legislative framework. This positive tone is challenged by Noble and Irwin (2009), who suggest that the emphasis on agency targets, efficiencies, and outcomes can squeeze out the relationship-based aspects of practice and in doing so can lead to the marginalization of the emotional and therapeutic aspects of practice (Bogo and McKnight, 2006). Bamford (1982) suggests that supervision can impinge on the autonomy of workers and the managerial function is that aspect of supervision where the power swings from the worker to the organization. For Simon and Ela, this is a genuine issue. Simon will be in part representing the organization and will be required to examine Ela's practice in line with organizational remits and aims. In the context of this book, it would be easy to look upon this aspect of supervision as unwelcome, but it is of course a crucial part of upholding standards and efficacy of practice.

Ingram (2013c) found that when social workers felt disinclined to bring the emotional aspects of their practice to supervision, they often cited a sense that it would not be seen by their agency as robust or meaningful and that a procedural casework approach would be more comfortable. However, for some social workers there was a congruency between the management functions of supervision and the place of emotions. It should also be noted that some social workers experience a sense of safety and comfort in a supervisory relationship that sticks to the procedural and practical content of practice. This may be due to the inevitable vulnerability associated with sharing and exploring complex and possibly previously less conscious aspects of one's practice. This again reminds us that the focus of supervision requires the engagement and commitment of supervisor and supervisee to avoid restrictive, collusive, and passive approaches to supervision.

We will examine this in more detail in Chapter 7, but it is clear that it is through the management function of supervision that the organizational culture and associated messages cascade down to the supervisory relationship. If we consider the impact of organizational culture on workers' emotional presentation (Hochschild, 1983), it is clear it will have an effect on the balance between the three aspects of supervision.

Learning activity

Consider your own supervision experiences and list the features that best fit under each of the three core functions (managerial, supportive and educational). Are there any features that do not fit well under these headings? If so, create a further heading to reflect the model of supervision as you see it.

It would be very useful for you to try this in conjunction with your supervisor to see where any similarities and differences lie. If you feel uncomfortable doing this task with your supervisor, then it may also be instructive to do it with a colleague to compare thoughts and share ideas.

Emotions and the supervisory relationship

It is tempting to reduce supervision to an activity that can be explained and performed simply by reference to a model or conception of what supervision should be. However, the element that brings life to these models and ultimately sets the tone and content is the *participants*. In the context of the typical conception of supervision, the participants are the supervisee (practitioner) and supervisor (senior member of staff/line manager). This relationship is subject to a range of variables, including responsibilities, agendas, personalities, power differences, pressures, and resources. This list is not exhaustive but hints at the potential variability of experience from one supervisory relationship to another, and underlines the importance of not being complacent about what supervision *should* be.

The relationship between supervisor and supervisee in many ways mirrors practice relationships in that the key hallmarks of a positive supervisory relationship are trust, support, and empathy (Noble and Irwin, 2009). O'Donoghue and Tsui (2011) noted that although supervisors were rather eclectic in the way they approached supervision, they often reported that they drew substantially on their own social work skills base to help them navigate the process. This is helpful for the purposes of this book, as it points to the place that relationships and emotional intelligence occupy within the relationship. Ingram (2013d) established the links between emotional attunement and the development of trusting and genuine relationships in social work practice. It is these qualities that must be drawn upon here. If we accept this as an important aspect of supervision, then it becomes clear that the emotional content of practice is central to this relationship.

Smith (2000) noted than when social workers asked what quality the 'ideal supervisor' ought to possess, a common response was to 'be there' for them. This simply means that social workers want their work (whether explicitly successful or complex and difficult) to be valued and validated. This does not mean a passive non-critical acceptance, but one that opens up an environment in which the complexities of practice can be explored and the practical and emotional aspects of practice can be brought into focus. This is essentially about creating an enabling and reflective environment. It is important to remember that this is not a 'blue sky' aspirational goal for supervision, but one that is highlighted as essential within the PCF (College of Social Work, 2012) in terms of developing autonomy and critical analysis, and also is echoed by Munro (2011) in relation to the complexities of relationships in practice. Ruch (2012: 1322) neatly encapsulates why the emotions and relationships within practice cannot be reduced to procedures and outcome measures, when she notes that 'within social work practice . . . the non-negotiable dimension of the task is the central place of human beings'.

Voices of practitioners: Olivia, criminal justice social worker

'Safety depends on your supervisor and how they view supervision . . . My last two, they were fine about emotions, but as social workers we need to back it up with something else. The safety issue is about covering your back so that you have done all the checks so that you are responsible for your own practice.'

Olivia echoes the notion that the individual supervisory relationship is crucial. This may be in terms of individual approaches to the concept of supervision, as well as in terms of the nature and quality of the relationship between the two participants. I use the word 'participants' hesitantly, as it might suggest a sharing of control and power in terms of the focus of supervision. This is not reflected in the response of most social workers, who view the quality and remit of their supervisory relationships as something they experience and respond to rather than co-create. Olivia also places the discussion of the emotional aspects of practice in the sphere of defensibility and presentation of practice. This is linked explicitly to the issue of safety, and the core of her argument appears to be that it would be *unsafe* to make decisions and present your practice without identifying the role of emotions. This appears to hint at good reflective practice rather than being about the removal of emotions. It is in circumstances where this is not permitted that reflection and clarity of actions become uncertain.

Ingram (2013c) asked social workers about their experiences of supervision and the extent to which they were able to explore the emotional content of their practice. What emerged was a highly variable picture but one that showed that the quality of the relationship with the supervisor was crucial. An overarching theme was that when supervision was deemed *not* to be conducive to exploring emotions, the issues of 'safety' and 'permissions' were often cited as key factors. The word 'safety' is a powerful one, in that by association it brings into play the idea of *danger*. This seems rather at odds with our preceding discussion about the qualities required of a positive reflective supervisory relationship. Figures 6.1 and 6.2 illustrate the differing interpretations that an emotionally inclusive supervisory relationship versus one that raises concerns about safety can have on what a social worker shares in supervision.

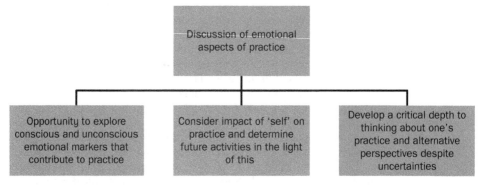

Figure 6.1 Supervision in which it is deemed safe to discuss emotions

Figure 6.2 Supervision in which it is deemed unsafe to discuss emotions

These two figures illustrate the powerful impact that differing interpretations of supervision can have on the experience of social workers. In relation to Simon, he will have a significant role in setting the tone and culture for his relationship with Ela. It is evident that Ela may feel vulnerable in terms of expressing and exploring the challenges of her caseload. If we consider the socially constructed aspects of emotions discussed in Chapter 1 (Turner and Stets, 2005), then it is essential that Simon draws on the qualities suggested by O'Donoghue and Tsui (2011) to let Ela know that he is willing and able to tune into her emotional world and value the blurred aspects of her practice. Given the potential for such complexities to be funnelled towards the health and well-being arena, it is important that Simon also makes explicit the permission for exploring such issues without risk of negative appraisal (Hair, 2012). The issues in relation to Elizabeth's practice learning supervision are slightly different. On the one hand, the educational function of this supervisory relationship should allow for learning, uncertainty, and development. However, Simon will need to consider the implications of his role as assessor (in many ways not unlike the complications inherent in the duality of the supervisor/line manager roles) of Elizabeth's practice. This may force Elizabeth to feel that sharing any doubts and uncertainties will be perceived as 'not knowing'. This is a subtle but powerful distinction and unless explicitly addressed and agreed between Simon and Elizabeth, may lead to suppression and editing of the emotional content of practice. This potential tension underpins the common practice of establishing a contract between supervisor and supervisee in the context of practice learning (Doel, 2009). This takes the student out of the role of passive recipient of whatever supervisory style the supervisor prefers, and into one that is at least explicit and preferably negotiated. Hafford-Letchfield (2009) notes that this co-production of supervisory focus can be extrapolated to qualified supervision also.

Learning activity

- Do you have experience of using contracts to underpin supervision? Why did you adopt this approach? What was contained within them?
- What might the challenges be when developing an agreement in partnership with a supervisor? What would you wish a contract to include that highlights the role of emotions in practice?

Developing a supervisory partnership

It is hard to argue with the notion that the supervisory relationship involves a degree of co-production and agreement (albeit within the context of agency function, remit, and goals). What is more difficult still is genuinely achieving such an outcome. The reason for this is unavoidably linked to issues of power, but is also subject to the variables noted at the outset of this chapter, such as limited resources and outcome/target focused approaches. Jindal-Snape and Ingram (2013) proposed a model of co-produced supervision (within the context of doctoral supervision) that required supervisors and supervisees to plot their desired content of supervision on a horizontal and vertical axis. Ingram (2013c) developed this in the context of emotions and supervision. In Figure 6.3, this model is adapted and developed further to identify the key areas of discussion and debate that must underpin such an agreement. It can be seen that the plotting of the proposed focus of supervision allows both parties to see where there is common ground and also where there is any divergence of expectations. Any meaningful discussion about the content and balance of supervision needs to take into account the contextual factors listed in Figure 6.3. For example, the organizational expectations of supervision need to be explicit (possibly even plotted on the same axis). This will flag up associated variables such as agency targets, impact of resources, and role and remit of workers. If any of these elements is overlooked at this stage, then the foundations are incomplete at best and doomed to failure at worst.

This sets in motion a process of discussion, negotiation, and agreement that is fluid and requires ongoing evaluation and review (see Figure 6.4). The quality and importance of the relationship between supervisor and supervisee are key to this process, as the quality of the process is dependent upon that relationship.

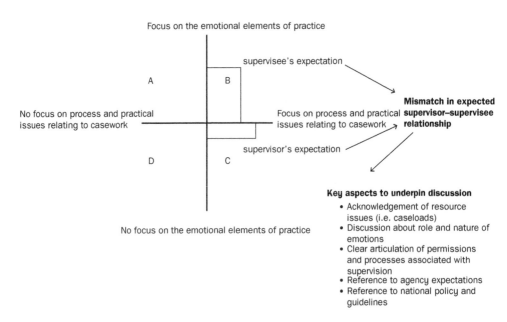

Figure 6.3 Plotting the balance of the content of supervision in partnership

Source: Adapted from Jindal-Snape and Ingram (2013) and Ingram (2013c)

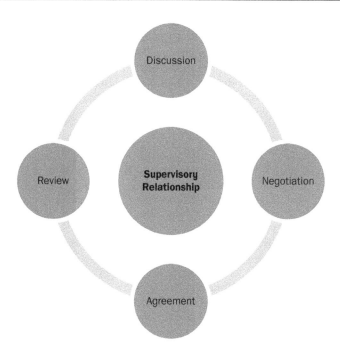

Figure 6.4 The place of the supervisory relationship in the development of an agreed approach to supervision

This underlines the need for both participants to be proactive both at the inception of the supervisory relationship and moving forward (as the aforementioned pressures and variables will inevitably challenge the agreement at times). This has been rather process-driven so far, and runs the risk of overlooking the inter- and intra-personal aspects of such discussion, particularly given the focus on emotions. I suspect that many readers will be finding it hard to envisage easily engaging in such co-produced activities. O'Donoghue and Tsui (2011) note that within the context of supervision in New Zealand, there is increasing awareness that supervisors must 'get to know' their supervisees in terms of their backgrounds and experiences to help support genuine engagement within supervision. This brings us back to the need for the supervisory relationship to mirror and utilize the skills and qualities required within practice relationships. O'Donoghue and Tsui (2011) describe this knowledge about 'how' to do supervision in addition to the more familiar knowledge about 'what' supervision is. Hennessey (2011) helpfully reminds us that gender, age, sexual orientation, and ethnicity are all factors that can impact on the supervisory relationship, and as such should be identified and discussed from the outset to achieve as transparent and empowering a forum as possible.

Alternative models for emotionally inclusive supervision

The preceding discussion has highlighted a range of opportunities and challenges within the context of social work supervision. The many alternative conceptions of supervision are beyond the remit of this book, but it is helpful to identify some key examples that may enhance the ability for supervision to usefully incorporate the emotional content of practice.

Noble and Irwin (2009) suggest that the increasing emphasis on the managerial functions of supervision has acted as a catalyst for seeking and developing opportunities for the therapeutic and reflective elements to be safeguarded in other arenas. They note that to achieve this, social workers benefit from working within a learning culture that allows such activities to be developed (Gould and Baldwin, 2004). Put simply, the willingness and permissions of an organization to establish a range of forums for support and guidance outside the familiar formal supervisory relationship are key.

Clinical supervision

Bogo and McKnight (2006) highlight the potential role for clinical supervision of social workers. Clinical supervision has as its prime focus the inter- and intra-personal dynamics of practice and associated relationships. For such an environment to be created, it is often explicitly separated from the line management functions of an organization (these can be contained within a parallel system of support). Beddoe (2010) highlights an emerging approach in New Zealand that involves supervision being provided externally to the agency, which enhances the sense of 'safety' to engage in reflective discussion without the perception of managerially driven judgements and priorities. Hair (2012) notes a similar trend in Swedish social work, in which workers receive reflective supervision external to the agency and administrative supervision within. Gibelman and Schervish (1997) note that clinical supervision may also be protected from the resource pressures of case priorities and limited time that can beset formal supervision. This seems very attractive on many levels given our preceding discussion of the potential power issues inherent in the supervisory relationship. Beddoe, however, issues a note of caution in that out-sourcing supervision in this manner may create a divide between the agency and worker and confusing and competing messages may emerge. Even more fundamentally for the purposes of this book, it may further marginalize emotions in relation to the core business of social work agencies, and in a sense 'keep them out there' as something extracurricular.

Ingram (2013a) found pockets of clinical supervision within the UK context, which was linked to the nature and complexity of particular social work tasks (i.e. child sexual abuse). Social workers found such supervision immensely supportive and beneficial but also recognized that in a sense it was divorced from procedural discussions with supervisors, and was very closely aligned with their health and well-being rather than locating their reflections and emotions *within* the discussions of the practice. Thomas and Spreadbury (2008) use the term 'professional supervision' interchangeably with clinical supervision. This is helpful for this discussion, as it underlines that to engage in reflection about one's emotions, values, and actions is to be professionally accountable in terms of one's practice and professional registration (GSCC, 2004; SSCC, 2004). This not only highlights the importance of professional development and accountability, but also powerfully locates this in wider professional terms than simply within agencies and organizations. This will provide a backbone to any discussion between Simon and Ela about the content of supervision between them, while also perhaps highlighting that a division between formal and clinical supervision could ameliorate the potential difficulties that Ela may have in terms of feeling able to talk about the complexities of how she feels about her practice.

The use of mentoring may provide a means for support to be offered that is separated (at least in part) from line management responsibilities (Donnellan and Jack, 2010). The mentoring relationship is characterized by an emphasis on support and guidance. It is located most commonly in the context of learning and development, and the seniority of the mentor to the mentee is about depth of experience rather than management responsibilities. This fits well with the concept of the learning practitioner (SSSC, 2008). For these arrangements to genuinely make the leap from formal supervision to a safe and different environment, the purpose, function, and feedback loops to the organization need to be explicit and agreed. Where this is fudged or overlooked, the potential for it to quickly mimic formal supervision in terms of overlaps with management and agency function is heightened.

Group supervision

So far, much of our discussion has centred on supervisory relationships that involve two key participants: a supervisor and supervisee. Bogo and McKnight (2006) identify the richness that can found in supervision that is conducted within a wider group of colleagues and peers. They make explicit and highly relevant links to the wider literature on group theory and group work practice (see Doel, 2006; Doel and Kelly, 2013). This echoes the useful links between one-to-one supervision and literature relating to relationship-based practice. A list of the benefits of receiving (at least some) group supervision include:

* sharing experiences with colleagues 'in the same boat'
* exploring complexities of practice with the strength of a collective voice
* providing mutual support
* sharing knowledge and resources
* engaging with a range of perspectives.

Lomax et al. (2010) note that in keeping with effective group work practice, it is important that such supervisory arrangements are underpinned by ground rules that help manage the potential challenges of generating diverse views and perspectives. In addition, the ground rules must make explicit the balance of the managerial, supportive, and educational aspects. These cannot be taken as a given. It is evident that sharing the emotional content of one's practice with colleagues may be therapeutic and helpful, but as we will see in the next section of this chapter, this may be taken up in less formal forums.

Thomas and Spreadbury (2008) note a middle ground in which group support can have a semi-formal status. They identify groups that can be formed to meet particular needs or focus (e.g. a group to provide peer support for workers from minority groups). They identify the strength and power of developing a collective voice to impact on organizational change. They note that such a collective voice emerges from reflective and safe discussions rooted in 'communities of practice' where shared experiences are examined. In the context of emotions, it is clear that the confidence and insight gained through group discussion may help to shape the organizational culture that has already been highlighted as being so crucial to the quality and nature of formal supervision.

Learning activity

* Have you been a member of formal or informal groups of practitioners/students formed to address specific issues/topics?
* Were these effective in meeting your needs? If so, why? If not, what were the limitations?
* Can you identify other groups within your organization (or perhaps more widely) that offer support and guidance to colleagues?

Support and guidance from peers and colleagues

This chapter has focused largely on formal arrangements and opportunities for support and supervision. You may of course have an enormously rich and helpful support network available simply through your relationships with colleagues. Ingram (2013c) asked social workers to identify the most useful and commonly used forum for support and guidance, and that which came out on top was 'informal support from colleagues'. Donnellan and Jack (2010) asked a similar question to newly qualified social workers and found that support from colleagues was ranked equally with formal supervisory arrangements.

Noble and Irwin (2009) note that seeking support from colleagues may be a response to the emphasis on management approaches detracting from the therapeutic aspects of supervision in which emotions may be explored. This is one explanation, but Ingram (2013c), Donnellan and Jack (2010), and Thomas and Spreadbury (2008) indicate a range of other factors that can be developed further in relation to the exploration of the emotional content of practice (see Box 6.1).

Box 6.1: Features of support from colleagues

Features of informal support from colleagues	Influence on the ability to explore, reflect, and examine the emotional aspects of social work practice
Timing and availability	Support from colleagues can be accessed 'on the spot' rather than waiting for a pre-arranged formal supervision session. This may allow issues to be explored as they arise and in turn feed back into ongoing practice.
Shared experience	The potential for colleagues having experienced similar issues within their own practice allows for a sense of empathy and acceptance. This also fosters the development of 'practice wisdom' among colleagues.
Unrecorded	The informality of such interactions means that the complexities of practice can be explored and 'tested' out with an arena that may involve appraisal and management. This may address the aforementioned issues of 'safety' in supervision.
Preparation for formal supervision	Discussion with colleagues can provide opportunities for reflection, helping to unpick the complexities of practice and in turn allow social workers to form a clearer sense of their role and understanding prior to supervision.
Enhanced sense of belonging	The opportunity to share ideas with colleagues may help social workers to develop a team culture that is conducive to exploring emotions and may impact on the more formal aspects of an organization. This may also be supported by actively 'looking out for each other', rather than it being a unidirectional support system.

Box 6.1 provides a strong argument for highlighting the role of support from colleagues. It is of course vulnerable and variable depending on the nature and size of the organization in which you find yourself. It is also worth noting that the features of availability and safety noted above will be dependent on environmental factors, such as office configuration and associated opportunities for contact and/or privacy. It is certainly worth reflecting upon the way office space and team arrangements within the context that you operate may facilitate or impinge on your ability to access informal peer support. The mechanics of establishing a learning culture will be covered in Chapter 7 when we look more closely at organizations, but Hafford-Letchfield (2009) notes that the informal peer-led aspects of this are as much part of the picture as the formal constructed aspects. If we consider the importance of prevailing cultures on how emotions are labelled and expressed (Turner and Stets, 2005), we can see why social workers may value stepping outside of the formal arenas of support and supervision to allow for a potentially less articulate and unguarded exploration of the emotional content of practice. It is of course worth noting that the quality of the support and advice of colleagues may be rather variable, and the potential dangers of unaccountable and unrecorded support leading to mixed messages for social workers have been noted (Beddoe, 2010). This underlines how such informal systems of support work best when allied to more formal arrangements as part of a wider positive reflective learning culture.

Voices of practitioners: Steve, an adult care team manager

'I have a trusted colleague with whom I can exchange weaknesses . . . a bit like a problem shared is a problem halved. I am not looking for solutions but just being able to say "this is a bloody hard situation and I am struggling" . . . can release the pressure . . . you need that because of the emotions in the job and if you are not getting the back-up from the system, you need to find it elsewhere . . . it is also because it is not minuted.'

Steve highlights that one of the key benefits of sharing the emotional content of your practice with colleagues is that there is a sense that they will know of and have experienced similar issues within their own practice. This clearly allows practice wisdom to be shared, but also may go some way to addressing the issue of safety, as there is an implicit or explicit recognition that these issues are valid and are part of the experience of being a social worker. The comment about the 'un-minuted' nature of such discussions is a crucial one and sets it apart from more formal mechanisms such as supervision or formal meetings. The idea that an un-minuted discussion is attractive clearly has links to the issue of 'feeling safe', and also suggests a potentially covert approach to discussing emotions. This covert approach to emotions chimes with previous discussion in relation to the suppression or removal of emotions from recording practice.

Learning activity

- What opportunities for informal support from colleagues have you experienced in your practice?
- Has this been useful? If so, what was it that was useful?
- How would you rank formal supervision in relation to support from colleagues?

Key learning points

- The role of supervision is not fixed and can be multi-functional. This can facilitate and/or impede the discussion of the emotional content of practice.
- The content of supervision is strongly influenced by the relationship between supervisor and supervisee. An open and transparent dialogue about what the focus of supervision should be is required to clarify permissions and expectations.
- Social workers value opportunities to reflect and explore the less certain aspects of their practice.
- Informal support from peers is enhanced by a sense of shared experience.

Further reading

Agass, D. (2002) Countertransference, supervision and the reflection process, *Journal of Social Work Practice*, 16 (2): 125–33.
This paper focuses on the inter- and intra-personal dynamics present in a supervisory relationship.

Kadushin, A. and Harkness, D. (2002) *Supervision in Social Work* (4th edn.). New York: Columbia University Press.
This is a comprehensive account of the many approaches and conceptions of social work supervision.

7 Organizational culture and emotions

Chapter objectives

This chapter will:

- Examine the terms 'managerialism' and bureaucracy to establish a clear sense of their place within organizations and how they may impact on emotions and individual experiences.
- Consider models of organizations and how these may impact on how individuals experience organizations and can contribute to them.
- Identify the links between the concept of 'learning organizations' and the development of organizational cultures that encourage individual reflection and development.
- Develop a clear understanding of how wider narratives about the social work profession can help to embed the centrality of emotions within organizations.

Emotions and organizational culture: setting the scene

It is intuitive to think about the emotional aspects of social work in the context of relationships and experiences at an *individual* level. In the preceding chapter on supervision and support, we began to think about how you might be given opportunities to think about and use your emotions. What is perhaps less immediately evident is the central role that the organizational culture and context that you find yourself within can have on your ability and opportunity to engage with the emotions and practice. Linking back to Chapter 1, we can begin to identify how the socially constructed elements of our conceptual framework of emotions can be brought into play (i.e. rules and norms) to help us unpick and understand organizational culture. We will explore a range of organizational contexts, which will highlight that in certain circumstances organizations can focus more on the procedural mechanics of social work at the expense of the human elements such as experiences, emotions and achievements (Hafford-Letchfield, 2009).

Anecdotally, I have found that when social work students write about their practice, they tend to focus their attention on the details of their individual practice. When they seek to address wider influences on their practice, they tend to highlight the role of legislation, policy, and theory (Dowson et al., 2010). What is less evident is the impact of the organization in which they are placed. Coulshed and Orme (2006) would argue that this is a serious omission, as they suggest that organizations are in effect a product of the people contained within in them. They suggest that the people within organizations abide by and contribute to the development of certain rules, hierarchies, and processes. Without such tacit agreement (whether passive or active), organizations simply fail to function. Indeed, Senior and Loades (2008) suggest that perhaps organizations can best be understood by viewing them as individually experienced phenomena. That is, organizations are part of our external environment and are understood through the lens of our own experiences and perspectives. This suggests that as social workers we must think about our organizations as part of who we are as practitioners and, in the context of this book, how and if the emotional elements of our practice are experienced and used.

In this chapter, we will explore a range of perspectives about how organizations are constructed and function, and in turn what this means for the role of emotions in social work. In their seminal book *In Search of Excellence*, Peters and Waterman (1982) provide us with a strong message that whatever the structure of an organization, those that function best are those that value, engage, and motivate their workforces. We will look at how this may be achieved within the social work context and how you can make an impact on what may at first appear to be something unwieldy and beyond your immediate sphere of influence. Senior and Loades (2008) note that with the emergence of professional registration, there is an opportunity and need for social workers to think about how their organizations facilitate or compromise their ability to fulfil the requirements of registration (GSCC, 2004; SSSC, 2004). Indeed, even the most cursory glance at the Professional Capabilities Framework (PCF; College of Social Work, 2012) will reveal the repeated reference to the importance of understanding and engaging with the organizational context in which one works. The need for congruence between the values and ethics of the social work profession within organizations is a key theme. This chapter will help you navigate the potential challenges inherent in managerially focused organizations, and look at the wider professional narratives about autonomy and professional judgement.

The following case study will help you to make links between our discussion about organizational culture and emotions and your own practice contexts, past or present.

Case study

Fiona is a postgraduate social work student on the final practice learning opportunity of her qualifying Master's programme. She has been placed within a voluntary sector homeless unit. One of the modules she must complete involves identifying a learning need within the organization, and in turn delivering a training event to contribute to the development of her colleagues and peers. She is required to identify the learning need through a process of consultation and negotiation with her colleagues. This process is then followed by a period of individual research into the topic and a planning phase in which she will consider the organizational culture, resources, and arrangements that will impact on how/when/where she delivers the training event.

Fiona initially found her colleagues to be resistant to the idea of identifying a potential training need. They cited how busy the unit was and that they were also struggling to identify a learning need that required addressing. This was echoed by management, who suggested that Fiona think of something herself, and time would be found at a staff meeting for her presentation. Fiona felt rather deflated, as many of her peers received a great deal of cooperation in their practice learning contexts. She persevered and sent an online questionnaire to her colleagues, acknowledging that people were busy and the questionnaire could be completed at a time that suited

them. The response rate was good and the topic of emotional intelligence and rela-
tionships with residents was identified as a learning need.

Fiona embarked on a substantial amount of research and was able to negotiate
with management to set aside time devoted to the 'event'. The training event was well
attended and evaluated by the staff of the organization. Many attendees noted that it
was refreshing to discuss such issues and that they felt that it was highly relevant to
their on-going practice.

Learning activity

- What might the response be to such a process in the organization that you currently practise within (or a previous practice context)? What does this tell you
  about the organizational culture in terms of learning and development?
- How might Fiona feel as she struggles to gain support for the idea of a training
  event? Should she try to address any organizational barriers? If so, why and how?

Emotions, managerialism, and bureaucracy: towards compatibility

It is difficult to mention the words 'managerialism' and 'bureaucracy' without immediately provoking negative connotations and responses from social workers. These two
words are often highlighted as the nemesis of autonomous and creative practice, and can
be seen to be an impediment to the 'core business' of social work practice and relationships. I would suggest that for social work as a profession, an ethical and values orientation alerts social workers to potential power imbalances and/or removal of human
self-determination and inclusion. This feeds into the distrust that can develop around the
purpose and intention of organizations (Donnellan and Jack, 2010). As noted earlier, this
approach to thinking about organizations is too one-dimensional, as individual workers
cannot meaningfully disentangle themselves from being *part* of what the organization is.
Additionally, if we consult the PCF (College of Social Work, 2012), it will become immediately apparent that there is a professional expectation that social workers need to
actively engage with their organizations across the domains of the framework.

Ferguson (2003) notes that the aforementioned deficit approach to thinking about
management and bureaucracy can be unhelpful and may overlook the positive and necessary functions associated with it. Senior and Loades (2008) state that while organizational management *can* involve the targeting of resources and strategic purpose (both of
which are important and create a welcome environment for accountability and scrutiny),
it is also possible for these wider aims and the individual workers to be brought together.
This opens the door for thinking less about the dangers of managerialism and more about
the potential opportunities. It may be useful at this point to make links with Chapter 6,
which examined the need for supervision to move beyond a focus on outcomes and
efficiency. In the next section, we will examine more closely the types of organization
that facilitate a greater focus on the individual and in turn their emotional (as well as
practical/procedural) experience of social work. Again, if we consider the strategic
capabilities contained within the PCF, there is explicit reference to the need for social work
management to inspire, motivate, and value social workers. This is linked to research,

collaboration, and learning, and provides a vivid example of the potential for management to help facilitate emotional awareness and self-knowledge.

Ruch (2012) highlights the difficult balance that needs to be struck between the rigidity and apparent simplicity of seeing social work as a procedural activity than the complex and emotionally charged reality of social work practice. Given the discussion in the preceding paragraph, it is possible to see this as a *balanced* rather than an *either/or* type of debate. If we return to the work of Hochschild (1983) and the suggestion that organizations can provide such persuasive cultures and rules for workers that they learn to express and (in some cases) feel emotions in line with organizational expectations, then there would be a significant cause for concern (see Chapter 1). However, follow-up research by Bolton and Boyd (2003) found that workers were able to find space for their own emotional self despite strong organizational messages about the right way to feel and behave. That is, workers draw on more than the immediate environment and look to other sources such as previous experiences, professional values, personal values, and motivations. This feeds into the argument that social workers can/should find opportunities to locate their own emotional worlds within organizations. As we will see later in the chapter, there are organizational constructs that help make this easier; however, the emotional labour of practice will exist regardless of whether it is captured in concrete bureaucratic policies and procedures or not (Mann, 2004; Ruch, 2012).

Bureaucracy most often refers to the structures, rules, and procedures that provide a framework for organizational behaviour and activities. Ferguson (2005) notes that bureaucratic solutions are often sought in response to high-profile tragedies in social work at the expense of considering the emotional worlds of the practitioners who operate within organizations. This chimes with Weberian conceptions of bureaucracies, which seek to reduce operations to procedures and processes and overlook (or indeed actively eliminate) the role of the humans involved. The gold standard here is one of efficiency and predictability. This approach to bureaucracy has a less neat fit with social work owing to the fundamental fluidity and potential 'messiness' of human relationships and behaviour (Aldridge, 1996; Senior and Loades, 2008). Beddoe (2010) echoes this notion within the context of risk, and emphasizes that strict procedures can severely limit the opportunity for the self-determination of service users (i.e. taking manageable risks) and professional judgement of social workers. If we return briefly to our conceptual framework proposed in Chapter 1, and the central role that emotional responses play in the way we react and interpret meaningful events, we can begin to make a claim for emotions and 'self' having an influence on choices and decisions within the context of procedures. Furthermore, it could also be argued that rules and procedures provide a necessary framework and structure to ensure consistency, accountability, and safety on the part of social workers and those who use social work services (Hafford-Letchfield, 2009).

Figure 7.1 presents a typical hierarchical organizational structure that shows the power and control in the hands of a few individuals at the top, with the majority of workers further down the hierarchy. This model is important, as it reminds us of how stark hierarchical power structures can be and more importantly how rigid and static they can appear. Coulshed and Orme (2006) note that such a pyramid-type structure tells us nothing about where an organization is going strategically, or the complex human relationships and emotions contained within. However, it is important that we begin to think of organizations more broadly than the rigid pyramid in Figure 7.1. This will help us to reduce our natural antipathy towards perceived power issues associated with such hierarchies. For those familiar with such pyramid structures, it is not uncommon for there to be reference to service delivery in the space below the pyramid. I have consciously omitted this in order to draw attention to the potential insularity of such structures. Given

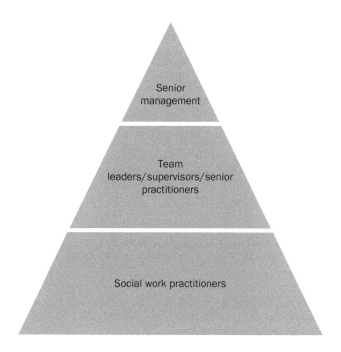

Figure 7.1 Typical pyramid hierarchical structure of organizations

such a structure, one can imagine how difficult it is for users of services to have an impact on the focus and direction of organizations.

The module task that Fiona has been asked to complete while on her practice learning opportunity is in line with the requirement embedded in the benchmarks for social work qualifications to engage with the learning needs of yourself, your colleagues, and the organization in which you operate (GSCC, 2004; SSSC, 2004). These are then picked up and echoed in post-qualifying frameworks such as the PCF (College of Social Work, 2012). For example, under the domain of 'Professional Leadership', it is stressed that social workers must actively seek and engage in learning and research alongside colleagues and wider networks. This provides Fiona with a framework if she finds her organization resistant to the idea of training and learning events. Similarly, Senior and Loades (2008) highlight that professional registration also provides social workers with leverage to engage with their organizations to ensure that they are able to meet the requirements of registration (i.e. continued professional development and working in partnership with service users). Where an organization does not facilitate such facets of practice, the social worker has a clear framework to draw upon to push for change (though this is not to underestimate such a task). This is very helpful when thinking about the place of emotions in organizations, as it reminds us that the place of emotions, self, relationships, and reflection is embedded in a range of frameworks and narratives about the profession of social work (Scottish Government, 2006; DCSF, 2009; Munro, 2011; College of Social Work, 2012), and thus provides a strong message and backdrop to organizational culture. This will add greater weight to the validity of the topic selected by Fiona and more broadly the notion that the organization and *management* need to facilitate the individual development and growth of workers.

Voices of practitioners

Simone, a children and families social worker

'It would be the revolution of social work to have emotions recognized organization-ally. It is that far away . . . which is hilarious because we work with people every day.'

Pete, a criminal justice social worker

'The organizational culture of the council says they recognize that the job is stressful . . . and that they appreciate us . . . that is also a national message too . . . that is as far as it goes though . . . more about understanding about what we are going through rather than addressing it . . . the next level should be what they are going to do about it.'

Simone provides a very stark and unpromising view of the organizational culture in which she works. The idea that a 'revolution' would be required highlights not only the distance between the existing organizational culture and one that recognizes the emotional elements of practice, but also that profound action would be required (a revolution may suggest a 'bottom-up' approach) to impact on the organizational structures that provide the backdrop to her experiences.

Pete is more upbeat in his response and recognizes that his organization makes a link between emotions, stress, and valuing staff. This is of course a rather limited conception of emotions (health and well-being), revealing it as something that is negative and simply individually experienced. The link to national level narratives is insightful, and may provide part of the answer to his concern about what can be done to move from rhetoric to something that is embedded within the organization.

Tuning into organizational culture: locating emotions

In a study of the views of frontline social workers in England, Jones (2001) found that there was a strong sense that social workers felt unsupported, emotionally overwhelmed, and demoralized. Jones linked this despondent profile in part to the messages that social workers received from the *organizations* in which they worked, in terms of how they were trusted and valued. The findings of Ingram (2013a) do not mirror entirely the apparently beleaguered profile of Jones' study, but the impact of the teams and organizations in which social workers work on their experience of practice was clearly evident.

Ayre (2001) points to the external pressures that impact on the way social work organizations conceptualize and support practice. For example, he highlights that stories of child abuse within the media are reported as failings of the social work profession rather than as crime stories, as is typical in other European countries. This he contends leads to a proceduralist approach to child protection in which the relationship-based aspects of social work are marginalized and procedures are seen as the clearest and safest way of working. Munro (2011) challenges such organizational and policy responses by embracing the centrality of relationships with service users and the emotional elements of social work. This potentially provides a strong footing for social work to address the move towards managerialist approaches. As noted previously, we can draw conceptually on the work of Hochschild (1983) to understand that despite professional expectations driving emotional *presentation*, the emotional labour required to manage the dissonance with the *felt* emotion is ongoing. Ingram (2013a) notes that for some social workers, the messages they receive from their organization echo the proceduralist paradigm, whether explicitly or implicitly. For example, discussing the difficult emotional elements of practice can be interpreted as a health/well-being issue organizationally, and in turn counselling services may be established to explore these in a separate sphere from practice-focused support such as supervision. This reflects an organizational approach to the role of emotions in practice and is linked to the messages that social workers receive in terms of the validity and 'safety' of articulating their emotions.

McGregor (2006) proposed two constructs of organizations that are extremely useful when trying to tune into organizational culture and the place that the emotional content of practice may have:

- *Theory X* – this construct of organizations views workers as not being able to exercise autonomy or having the underpinning knowledge and expertise to contribute meaningfully to the development of the organization. In its simplest sense, it is rooted in the belief that workers are inherently lazy, and that, as a result, a strict direction, procedures, and policies are required to guide the activities and decisions of workers. The echoes of this theory can be seen in the tightening of regulations and processes to regulate and *routinize* social work practice.
- *Theory Y* – this construct of organizations views workers as positive, engaged, and forward-looking. This type of organization seeks to establish structures that allow space for innovation, creativity, and autonomy. This requires workers to be valued for their unique contributions and being given genuine opportunities to participate in the development of the organization. This theory resonates with the notion of professional autonomy and the role of emotions and values that underpin such practice. The helpful link to participation and learning chimes with the notion of the learning organization (Crossan et al., 1999).

Learning activity

- Can you compare Theory X and Theory Y with the organization you practise (or have practised) in?
- Identify which rules, procedures, and arrangements facilitated or compromised your involvement. Did these affect the way you felt valued?
- How is the place of emotions affected by this analysis? What factors might help to shift your organization to one that considers your individual experiences, values, and emotions?

Hafford-Letchfield (2009) suggests that organizations develop rules, roles, and procedures that are intended to achieve agreed goals. She identifies that a scientific approach to management has been evident in social work and uses the metaphor of a machine to illustrate how procedures can be developed to achieve goals and outcomes, at the expense of the human elements within an organization. Walton (2005) suggests that there is a tension in such a bureaucratic model of an organization, as the focus on the individual social worker and their experiences is lost and an environment of inspection and regulation prevails. Although this metaphor may overstate the lack of connection

Figure 7.2 Social work organizational culture machine model

between social work organizations and social workers, Figure 7.2 highlights the interlocking cogs that shape organizations.

In Figure 7.2, I have developed and adapted the metaphor of the organizational
machine. It indicates the relationship between organizational culture, supervision, and
practice. If we consider the issue of 'safety' and the articulation of emotions in supervision (Ingram, 2013a), it is clear that those respondents who felt it unsafe to explore emotions adapted their approach within supervision and the wider organization to present
themselves in a detached and procedural manner. This in part is a presentational issue,
but the complex picture that emerged about the role of emotions within the social worker/
service user relationship suggests that cultural messages cascade down to direct practice and lead to uncertainties in terms of the role and validity of emotions. The positive
aspect of this model is the interconnectedness of the cogs. This allows consideration of
the impact that emotional discourse in supervision could have on practice and in turn on
organizational culture. Similarly, if you apply the messages from this book about the
centrality of emotions in the context of your own direct practice, this will have an impact
on how you articulate your practice in supervision and to colleagues, which in turn will
impact upon the prevailing culture and norms of the organization. Finally, if the organization
accepts the messages about emotions and use of self within the above professional narratives, we can see how powerfully this may impact supervision and practice. Senior and
Loades (2008) emphasize that any machine-type metaphor for organizations must take
cognizance of the many emotions inherent in any grouping of people, and vividly describe
organizations as being 'a hotbed of emotional life' (p. 278). In effect, one must visualize
the individual and collective emotional responses and experiences of the workforce
constantly influencing the organizational identity, culture, and direction through
each interlocking cog. This moves away from top-down/bottom-up visual representations

of organizations to one that is multi-directional and interconnected. If we conceptualize social work organizations in this way, it is much easier to envisage how the influence of service users might be felt.

If we link to the case study above, we will see some of these issues being played out in practice. Fiona initially experienced resistance from her colleagues, who found it diffi-cult to engage with an opportunity for professional development, and a muted response from management. This likely reflects a group of workers who are unused to having the opportunity to develop their knowledge and influence the practice of the organization. The lack of a positive response from management may reflect a preference for driving developmental and enhancement opportunities from the top down, which is at odds with the aims of the module. Fiona may have been surprised to find herself in a position of having the potential to influence the organization, but once she commenced the negotia-tion phase of her module (via a survey) she began to generate ideas and motivation. Although I am hypothesizing here, you can see how the cogs of the organization began to turn. The agreement to focus on the use of emotional intelligence when forming relation-ships with residents has its roots in direct practice and will (as we know from our concep-tual framework) resonate with and be applicable across the organization as a whole. If we return to the visual metaphor of the interconnecting cogs, it is possible to envisage the event influencing how workers engage with residents and in turn how they describe and discuss their practice informally and in supervision. Additionally, given the power of social consensus and observation (Rosenberg, 1990), it is easy to envisage how such changes in approach can quicken the momentum and become part of the organizational culture.

Learning activity

Look at the three cogs in Figure 7.2. Can you identify whether and how messages about the role of emotions are channelled through these areas in your organization or one you have experience of working within? If that proves too difficult, feel free to think about other issues that may evolve in one of the three areas and then have an impact elsewhere.

Emotions and the role of learning cultures and organizations

Much of our discussion so far has focused on organizational structures and how they impact the place that emotions and the individual experiences of social workers have within organizations. We have begun to develop a sense that within any given structure there will emerge a distinct culture that is, by definition, a product (at least in part) of the individuals within the organization and that this culture will communicate and facilitate a range of norms, rules, opportunities, and permissions. If we link back to the conceptual framework proposed in Chapter 1, we can see how important cultural and contextual expectations are for how we experience, label, and express our emotions (Rosenberg, 1990). Rosenberg notes the importance of role-modelling and social consensus, and how this reinforces powerful cultural cues. Senge (1990) believes that this brings the individ-ual and the organization together in a shared vision and an active engagement in new learning. This is of course mirrored strongly in the PCF (College of Social Work, 2012).

In recent years, the notion of learning cultures has evolved and provides us with a useful framework to locate the place of emotions and self within social work organizations. SCIE (2004) proposed a range of features that underpin a *learning* organizational culture. The features of a learning organization detailed in Figure 7.3 appear especially cogent when linked to the discussion on supervision in Chapter 6, as they shed light on where the apparent inconsistencies in the experiences of social workers may lie. The idea that shared beliefs are important is in line with the view of organizations being underpinned by a shared vision (Rosenberg, 1990). Ruch (2012) notes that the competing influences of outcomes-focused public management approaches and the less measurable emotional elements of practice present social work managers with a difficult balancing act. This does not need to be a binary debate if there is a cultural shift, whereby the emotional and relationship-based elements of practice are explicitly agreed and shared as important at all levels. This would be further enhanced by the 'safe' exploration of practice, which would encourage consideration of alternative perspectives, and allow for mistakes and uncertainties to be contained (Cornish, 2011). The notion of leadership at all levels chimes with the aspiration for increased professional autonomy and trust that permeates national narratives about the profession (Scottish Government, 2006; Munro, 2011). Bamford (1982) provides a cautionary view of the aspiration for greater professional autonomy, by emphasizing that organizational factors such as resources and policy are ever present and provide both opportunities for and obstacles to autonomy.

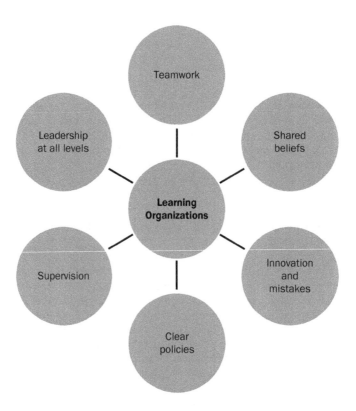

Figure 7.3 Characteristics of learning organizations

Murphy et al. (2013) present a sceptical analysis of whether relationship-based practice is genuinely achievable. A key strand of their argument is the impact of procedures, policy, legislation, and professional powers on genuine use of self within the context of emotions. This is a helpful point, as it helps ground any discussion about organizational culture in a realistic context.

Hafford-Letchfield (2009) reminds us that any discussion of a learning culture must acknowledge the formal (i.e. training and supervision) and informal (self-directed study and peer discussions) spheres. This is helpful because it allows us to think about organizations more broadly and not be constrained by an over-emphasis on the highly visible and structured aspects. This point was noted in relation to supervision in the previous chapter, in that informal support is a key aspect of a social worker's context. Similarly, learning can occur in a range of unprompted and informal arenas such as chance discussions about practice with colleagues within office spaces. This flexible and multifaceted approach to learning is highlighted in the post-registration training and learning requirement of newly qualified social workers in Scotland. Social workers are required to compile evidence of learning that can include formal learning such as training courses and less formal learning such as reflective accounts of pieces of practice. What is most encouraging about this is the explicit encouragement of learning, reflection, and development within qualified practice.

Marsick and Watkins (1990) define a learning organization as one that places all employees at the heart of organizational developments, which are underpinned by a shared vision and values. Kerka (1995) develops this further and notes that for this to be achieved, there needs to be a clear acceptance of individual difference and the potential for mistakes and complexities. Perhaps the idea of a *reflective* organization (Morrison, 2007) is also useful here, as it introduces the idea of a fluid organizational structure that, while forward-looking (learning culture), also brings in a cyclical learning approach that could allow for issues such as procedures, resources, and power to be constantly acknowledged and explored. Conceptually, these elements are part of the context in which individual workers will apply meanings to their emotions and regulate their expression. The model embraces these factors rather than hoping to remove them. Ingram (2013a) notes that among the participants in his interview study, a commonly expressed view was that they had not had an opportunity to consider the issues relating to emotions and practice prior to their involvement in the research. This may be a symptom of an organizational culture that has a strong managerialist flavour and one that does not focus on critical reflection and consideration of one's internal emotional world and/or the links with one's practice.

Crossan et al. (1999) developed a framework that helps us understand how an organizational learning culture may be achieved. They believe that ideas and perspectives are inherently individually generated. That is, organizations (as an entity themselves) do not generate ideas, individuals do. This links with the notion that social work is ultimately a human endeavour, understood and conducted in response to individually generated emotions, knowledge, and interpretations (Hennessey, 2011).

Crossan et al. (1999) proposed the '4 I's' framework, based on four key sequential stages:

- Intuition – ideas arise initially from individuals and may well develop from subconscious and pre-verbal stages into a verbal articulation. Such ideas will be framed by the individual's emotions, experiences, and values.
- Interpretation – this is the stage where ideas are expressed and then interpreted by others in the context of wider experiences and perspectives.

- Integrating – this phase is concerned with reaching a shared understanding across an organization about a particular issue or idea.
- Institutionalization – this is the point where the shared understanding is then developed into new processes and routinized within an organization.

The process described above sits comfortably with the notion of a learning organization in that the first three stages are fluid and involve ideas and critically reflecting upon uncertainties and complexities. This fluidity does not always result in organizational change and can simply represent an openness to learning and exploration. This is in line with the importance of organizations allowing the emotional content of practice to be considered and expressed individually and across organizations, and perhaps most crucially that there is space and acceptance for complexity and nuance.

This model also provides us with a framework to consider the current place of emotions within social work organizations. We have established the irrefutable centrality of emotions in the experiences and actions within practice. We have also noted the links between emotions and emotional intelligence in relation to service users and colleagues. Chapter 6 provides a clear depiction of the ways in which the *interpretation* and *integration* phases are commonplace in social work organizations. Current narratives about the profession of social work note the importance of emotions, reflection, and the importance of relationships. This in some ways fits with the fourth and final stage of organizational learning but requires the processes and structures to then follow suit and firmly embed emotions within social work organizations.

If we return to the case study, it is possible to understand the process Fiona undertook within this model. The intuition phase is already partly underway due to the formal structure and requirements of the academic module. However, it was through the use of a survey that Fiona was able to encourage and elicit ideas from a range of individuals within the team. The initial reticence of the team may underline how fluid and unplanned the intuitive phase can be and that it does not always result in tangible outcomes that can be taken forward. The integration phase was in some sense taken forward initially by Fiona who was charged (by module requirements) to research the topic and develop the content of the training event. It is also likely that the topic of emotional intelligence would have been interpreted and considered individually and collectively within the event itself as participants began to appraise the relevance of it to their practice experiences. The positive evaluations from participants suggest that, by the end of the event, there was a shared understanding and that participants could see the links to their work and the aims of the organization. I have already made links between Fiona's training event and the potential for organizational influence and change. If we accept that the messages about the use of emotions become part of the culture of the organization, it is possible that potentially new processes will emerge to reflect them (institutionalization).

Learning activity

- Reflect on your experiences (or those of others) of developing an idea that was then shared with colleagues. How does your experience fit with the 4 I's model? What are the cultural barriers to and/or facilitators of this process?
- How explicit are the messages contained within national narratives about the importance of emotions and use of self being cascaded down to organizational and individual levels?
- What can you do as an individual to enhance these messages?

Organizations, emotions, and collaborative practice

Our discussion about organizational culture and structure has largely focused on social work organizations in isolation. It would be easy to think of organizations and agencies as entities with impermeable walls that exist and develop in isolation from external factors and forces. This is of course not the reality of social work organizations or practice. It is difficult to imagine a practice context that does not require a certain degree of interdisciplinary collaboration. In some contexts, of course, this may be fully integrated into the structure of an organization (for example, unified Children Services departments). In other contexts, it will be about taking a holistic view of how separate organizations and professions contribute individually and collectively to the overall picture of service delivery. Either way, collaborative practice is a key aspect of the legislative, policy, and practice context of social work (Quinney, 2006).

Bronstein (2003) notes that interdisciplinary collaboration is ultimately an interpersonal process and phenomenon. Bronstein argues that it pushes professionals to consider their own values and perspectives in relation to the new and/or different professional orientations that one comes across when working with other professional groups. This ties in with the emphasis on the important role that individuals have in terms of organizational development (Crossan et al., 1999). That is, interdisciplinary collaboration creates an environment that necessitates new learning and gives rise to the need for self-reflection and clarity of one's own role. Bronstein (2003) highlights the need to create space for reflection when engaging in interdisciplinary collaboration, as one's sense of role and purpose is challenged and this has a significant emotional impact on workers.

The interdisciplinary nature of service provision creates an environment in which individual workers and the organizations in which they operate must develop personal and professional identities that are clearly distinct from other professions but flexible and fluid enough to meet the challenges of collaboration (Slay and Smith, 2011). This forces social workers to individually and collectively consider what the role and function of social work is. They are likely to draw on a range of sources, including research, literature, legislation, policy, codes of practice, and individual values. This process will involve the complex interplay of conscious and unconscious emotions as professional and personal identity evolves (Seden, 2011). This reflective process requires you to consider organizational culture (Rosenberg, 1990) and how this shapes how one appraises new professional challenges and orientations. The centrality of relationships and use of self are a core part of the social work identity (Ruch, 2012; Ingram, 2013d), and it is often this aspect that marks the profession out from others involved in collaborative service delivery. This presents an opportunity for social work to stake a claim for the importance of the emotional content of practice and underlines its place within professional identity and organizational culture.

Learning activity

Consider the other professional groupings that you currently or have previously worked with in practice settings. List the characteristics of these professions. This will involve identifying roles, remits, and approaches to practice. What are the similarities and differences in relation to social work? In your experience, what value do these professions place on use of self, relationships, and emotions?

Key learning points

- It was highlighted that social workers must think about and contribute to the organizations in which they practise. Organizations have rules, norms, and processes that impact upon all aspects of practice and in particular the emotional content of practice.
- Managerialism and bureaucracy were examined and space was identified for maintaining and valuing a sense of self within procedures and processes.
- Learning cultures were considered and the opportunities these present for managing and containing the complexities and uncertainties of practice were identified. The emergence of continuing professional development provides a helpful vehicle for learning and reflection to become part of organizational culture and activity.
- Theories of organizations were discussed to provide readers with a framework to tune into the organizational structures they work within.
- The increasingly interdisciplinary environment in which the social work profession functions was highlighted as an opportunity to further embed the role of emotions within the professional identity of social work.

Further reading

Gould, N. (2000) Becoming a learning organisation: a social work example, *Social Work Education*, 19 (6): 585–96.
This paper provides useful guidance and tips for actively creating an organizational environment that facilitates reflection and learning.

Hafford-Letchfield, T. (2009) *Management and Organisations in Social Work*. Exeter: Learning Matters.
This accessible book covers the key aspects of organizations and social work. It provides a useful resource for students and practitioners to start *thinking* about organizations.

8 | Emotions and the social work professional

Chapter objectives

This chapter will:

- Explore what is meant by the term professional and how this impacts on the image, perception, and reality of social work practice. Readers will be encouraged to consider how definitions of professionalism impact on their view of the compatibility of emotions and social work.
- Consider the notion of professional identity and how it is constructed and influenced by internal and external factors. The place that emotions have within the professional identity of social workers will be highlighted.
- The key themes for the book will be pulled together to contribute to the development of a model that locates emotions at the heart of what it is to be a social work professional. The proposed model will forge explicit links between professional frameworks, practice, organizational culture, and practitioner supports to create a vision of the profession that facilitates and accommodates the emotional aspects of practice within it. A key aspect of this model will be the removal of perceived barriers between these elements, which previously created a climate in which the emotional aspects of practice were seen as being in competition or incongruous with the technical-rational aspects of social work. The applicability and credibility of this model are enhanced through being underpinned by existing codes, policies, and narratives about the profession.

Emotions and the social work profession: setting the scene

The words profession, professionalism, and professionalization appear at regular intervals throughout this book. Often the notion of 'being professional' has appeared at odds with the acknowledgement that emotions play a central role within social work practice. This tension has, in part, been located within debates about the balance between rational-technical and relationship-based conceptions of the profession. In this chapter, we will explore in more depth the meanings that we apply to ideas of social work as a profession, and more broadly will examine what impact the term 'professional' has on the expectations, challenges, and opportunities for social work.

Readers of this book may be registered with a professional regulatory body. This is a statutory requirement of social workers in many counties globally, and in the UK is a requirement from beginning a social work qualifying programme through to the point of retirement. This sets social work students apart from many of their peers in higher education, as their academic degree programme is regulated and associated with a professional code of practice. This sets in motion a series of expectations and responsibilities associated with the qualification of social work. We will examine in more detail what this professional identity is and how emotions and use of self are a key component of this professional identity, both within the profession and in relation to other associated professional groupings.

The chapter will conclude with a model that establishes the place of emotions within a professional construct. This model will challenge the notion that there may be some incongruity with being professional and experiencing and using emotions. It will draw on a range of features of the profession to argue that emotions are in fact a valid and essential part of what it is to be a social work professional, and that perhaps it is this element that is *the* key aspect of the unique role that social work plays in a multidisciplinary practice context.

The following case study reintroduces us to Lorna from Chapter 2. She has now qualified as a social worker and is about to start her first job since graduating as a social worker. I have purposefully chosen to return to Lorna as she was initially uncomfortable with the interplay between academic study and the reflective/practice-based aspects of her social work programme. Having successfully completed her programme of study and achieved her *professional* qualification as a social worker, she will need to assess what is required and expected of her as a social worker and will likely survey the broad range of knowledge and experience she has garnered to help her make sense of what being a social work professional means.

Case study

Lorna has recently gained an undergraduate degree in social work. This degree qualifies her to work with the professional status of a social worker. She has recently changed her professional registration status from student to social worker. Lorna has thoroughly enjoyed her programme of study and feels ready to start her first job in a children and families team in a local authority.

Despite these feelings of confidence, she is also a little wary of the idea that she is now a qualified professional who will be making important judgements and decisions in partnership and on behalf of children and their families. Over the course of her programme, she has been able to engage with a broad range of theory and practice that will help her to undertake this role effectively. However, the media have recently reported a very high-profile and tragic child death, in which the poor judgement of a social worker has been deemed to be a pivotal contributory factor. This coupled with anecdotes from her colleagues makes her uncertain about how she will cope with the realities of her caseload and in turn how this may impact on her professional judgement. She is keen not to become a social worker that simply follows strict procedures and is still very committed to engaging with service users to work in partnership.

Professionalism: a complex concept

I suspect we all know what we mean by the words 'profession' and 'professional'. This sense of certainty about the terms gives us confidence to make judgements about what is professional and unprofessional. It allows us to calibrate whether a job had been done to a professional standard, or has dropped below such thresholds. The notion of professional judgement invokes a degree of importance and accuracy that lends it greater validity and weight. Phrases such as 'in my professional opinion' set such opinions apart for other less informed ones, and hint at a well of knowledge and expertise. Being told that 'you are rather unprofessional' may be perceived as a serious rebuke for a practitioner, and suggests that there are sets of acceptable pre-determined behaviours associated with the concept. In this section, we will explore some of these facets of the term, and highlight the impact this has on how we perceive social work and how this in turn strengthens or marginalizes the role of emotions.

Beckett and Maynard (2013) note that an important aspect of being a professional is that it moves beyond simply *being ourselves*. They identify a range of theory, legislation, policy and professional codes that shape and direct the content of what it is to be a social work professional. These influential codes of practice and ethics provide a visible and tangible set of standards and rules that mark out the territory of what is then judged to be within professional boundaries (GSCC, 2004; NASW, 2008; BASW, 2012b). Ingram et al. (2014) broaden this view of the social work professional further by highlighting that despite these frameworks and influences, we *do* bring our individual 'self' to bear on the professional we become. This suggests that the concept of the professional is about the *interplay* between universally shared frameworks and knowledge, with the skills, values, and emotions that we individually possess.

The term professional also carries with it notions of expertise and 'a job well done'. In the context of social work, this is linked to the aforementioned body of knowledge that underpins the profession, but also is about how this is actually used within practice. In many ways, it is the familiar 'theory to practice' axis that all social work students and practitioners have to engage with. The standards that are required of qualified social workers confer professional status. The Professional Capabilities Framework (College of Social Work, 2012) lays out a series of qualities that combine to create a vision of a social work professional. The following are a few selected ones that might helpfully identify the key themes involved:

- Having confidence in self and others
- Effective interventions
- Able to work in complex situations and seek opportunities for reflection
- Able to work autonomously and make high-quality judgements.

This brief sample from the PCF is useful, as it picks up on the notion that being a professional is about attaining a level of confidence and competence that is manifested in the actions one takes in practice. The focus is on the outcomes of professional practice and this is simply a mirror of the familiar notion of 'doing a good job'. This brings us to the measurability of effectiveness and reminds us that social work is at least partly characterized by a managerial outcomes-based focus and the ability of a social worker to be seen as 'professional' is tied up in such measures. It is also important to note that external evaluations of one's professionalism are most crucially made by service users in terms of the trustworthiness, genuineness, consistency, and effectiveness of the relationships they form with social workers. This creates a clear focus on the individual, their behaviour and ability to form relationships, and brings us back to the balance between the 'hard' and 'soft' aspects of the social work professional role (Ingram et al., 2014). The link between the complexity of practice and the need for reflection is helpful, as it builds the need for self-knowledge and critical reflection into what it is to be a social worker. In terms of this book and the conceptual framework proposed in Chapter 1, this is heartening, as it notes the importance of the intra-personal aspects of practice and in turn the need to consider one's emotional responses to achieve the required level of professionalism.

Voices of practitioners: John, a social worker with adults with learning disabilities

'I do not allow my feelings to dominate interactions (though they are not entirely absent) with service users, as I view my role as a professional one. This distance is required, particularly when difficult and at times conflicting decisions have to be made. It also serves to ensure that the service user knows throughout any interaction where they stand.'

In working with adults with learning disabilities, John held a rather mixed view of the role of emotions. He *did* view emotions as being compatible with the social work profession, but also felt able to ignore them at different stages within his practice. He concedes that emotions are likely to be present within his practice, but makes clear there is no relationship between their presence and the achievement of what could be viewed as professional practice. This separation is linked explicitly to the role of being a 'decision-maker' and echoes debates about the contested relationship between emotions and rational thoughts. It would appear that John is suggesting that emotions inhibit decision-making and it is the rationality of the decision-making that fosters professional status. There is also a sense that regulating emotions will create (professional) boundaries around the service user/worker relationship, in turn preparing the ground for making decisions that may conflict with the views of the service user. This provides an interesting link between relationship-based approaches and the balance with perceived professional boundaries.

Beckett and Maynard (2013) note that professionalism is not a static concept. They suggest it is a standard that social workers must constantly aspire to and one that can be compromised and challenged by competing forces. Fenton (2012) identifies the concept of 'ethical stress', which occurs when the organizational demands of an agency are at odds with one's professional value base. For example, an agency may demand that social workers limit the frequency and duration of visits to service users owing to high workloads and a quest for greater efficiencies. This will be at odds with a commitment to communicating respect and establishing effective relationships by taking time to establish them. This reflects a tussle to achieve professional standards when facets of the profession (organizational and individual) are competing with one another. This complex picture shows the need for ongoing professional development to constantly re-calibrate and enhance the standards that social workers must meet in the ever-changing world of practice (Wiles, 2013).

The following learning task is intended to get you thinking about what you perceive to be important elements of the concept of professionalism. It will encourage you to consider the nature and boundaries of ethical thresholds.

> **Learning activity**
>
> Consider the following examples from practice. First, note down whether you think each statement reflects a breach of what you feel to be professional. Once you have done that (you should be able to make a very quick judgement), list the reason for this and what it tells you about the component parts of being professional.
>
> - A social worker forms a very positive relationship with a service user. The social worker prioritizes meetings with this service user over others that are part of their caseload.
> - A social worker keeps in contact via social media with an ex-service user once they move to a new job.
> - A social worker agrees to 'keep a secret' during discussions with a 15-year-old female service user.
> - A social worker blames their organization for not providing adequate resources when offering a service to a service user.
> - Accepting gifts from service users.
> - Failing to challenge dangerous practice observed in the work of other social workers.
> - Basing a decision on 'gut feeling'.

This task will have raised a plethora of issues for you. These may have included the notions of professional boundaries and relationships; regulation of emotions; upholding standards; and the place of knowledge and evidence. What is crucial is that with very little prompting, we have created views about what constitutes 'being professional'. These reactions are drawn from our sense of what the social work profession means to us, and in turn our sense of professional identity. It is this concept to which we now turn.

Professional identity and social work

Professional identity is a 'self-concept', rooted in the values, motives, knowledge, and experiences of individuals engaged in professional practice (Ibarra, 1999). That is, it is what we feel and think as individuals about ourselves and our profession. This is an important concept, as it highlights that a profession cannot be encapsulated purely in a list of written codes, knowledge, roles, and remits, but is individually nuanced and experienced. This allows us to establish very clear links between the importance of self-knowledge when considering the role of emotions in social work and the notion of professional identity. Slay and Smith (2011) reinforce this link by stressing that professional and personal identity are intertwined. One draws on both streams of knowledge and experience when making judgements in practice and making sense of relationships and circumstances. This echoes the conceptual framework in Chapter 1 in that our emotional responses are influenced by previous experiences, prevailing cultures, and social norms. In a professional context, the culture and norms may be articulated within professional and organizational frameworks. If we accept this interplay between the personal and professional, then one of the central qualities of the social work profession in the use of self, and with it an absence of a 'one-size-fits-all' conception of what it is to be a social work professional. This is not to overlook the substantial and important frameworks, legislation, codes, and knowledge that contribute to professional identity, but simply that these are then combined with our individual qualities and experiences.

Arthur (2008) notes that the fluid nature of professional identity means that it is responsive to changing contexts and circumstances. Slay and Smith (2011) echo this by suggesting that professional identity evolves throughout one's career. This is in part highlighted in the PCF (College of Social Work, 2012) in the sense that it is recognized that professional capabilities develop with experience and are underpinned by continued learning and reflection. Slay and Smith (2011) suggest that professional identity can be scaffolded and enhanced by role-modelling. This brings us back to the importance of high-quality supervision and organizational commitment to learning (DCSF, 2009). It also underlines the power that prevailing cultures have on professional identity and the professional presentation that this then demands of workers (Hochschild, 1983). If we consider the case study, Lorna will be conscious that her professional identity is at an emerging stage as she makes the transition from student to qualified worker. She will sense that aspects of professional identity such as autonomy and accountability will increase during this transition. However, how this develops for her will be dependent also on the organizational context and culture in which she finds herself. What is important here is that Lorna's professional identity and experience of developing a sense of it will be unique to her, and will vary from that of her fellow graduates as they take their individual perspectives into differing social work environments.

It is clear from the preceding discussion that professional identity involves an interaction between the individual social worker and wider frameworks and knowledge bases that underpin the profession. However, we should not overlook the influence of the multidisciplinary context of social work practice and the associated impact that working with other professional groupings has on clarifying professional boundaries and purpose (Wiles, 2013). Frost et al. (2005) noted that significant learning occurs when working (practically and academically) alongside other professionals. Hannah et al. (2014) found that when social work students and educational psychology students worked together on a hypothetical case study, there was a blurring of professional identities as the overlaps and differences between the professions were highlighted and explored. It is usual for social work qualifying programmes to take account of the multidisciplinary world of practice, as to teach social work as if its role was isolated would be to fall short of the reality of practice. This wider context in which professional identity evolves is important, as it highlights that social work is a profession that is (unashamedly) responsive to other professions, service users, and bureaucracies (van Pelt et al., 2015). This responsiveness should not be viewed as a lack of focus or simply 'blowing with the wind'. It requires professional assertiveness and confidence to maintain a sense of professional identify in such a fluid context (Wilson et al., 2011).

This brings us to a key challenge for social work and its professional identity: is the profession and its wide-ranging remit and knowledge base too diffuse to achieve a coherent identity? Due to the generic aspects of the profession, the sources of knowledge and legislation can change dramatically from one practice context to another. A worker in a child protection setting may draw from a significantly different knowledge base than someone working in a criminal justice context. Of course, there will be many overlaps, but to an outsider they may appear entirely different careers. Part of the answer lies within the codes of practice, professional registration and education of social workers. However, it is similarly evident that a key aspect of the profession is the ability to draw from bodies of knowledge and information that are pertinent to each situation encountered in practice (Donnellan and Jack, 2010). This is rooted in the strongly held belief about recognizing the uniqueness and diversity of service users' lives and the meanings they apply to them. Rather than the apparent diffuse nature of social work being seen as a barrier to achieving a professional identity, perhaps we should argue that it is one of the core features of the professional identity of social workers. The ability to establish relationships, work in partnership with individuals across the life course, evaluate and manage risk, engage in critical reflection, and be accountable for one's decisions will vary from case to case and context to context. Van Pelt et al. (2013) suggest it is this fluid and reflective application of knowledge and professional role that constitutes a key part of the social work identity.

Learning activity

It is common to find oneself in the company of friends who have little or no knowledge of the social work profession. It is similarly common to find oneself trying hard to articulate a clear answer to the question, 'what is social work?'

Given the preceding discussion, list the features that best describe the identity of a social worker, such as 'a commitment to social justice'. Then try to identify how these features are manifested in practice situations with which you are familiar. Finally, try to identify the aspects of these practice contexts that are unique or at least central to the social work role.

The outcome of this task should equip you with a clearer sense of the values, knowledge, and skills associated with the professional and how these are then applied in practice – hence developing a professional identity.

To navigate one's way through this ever-changing professional identity, it is essential that social workers are engaged with and open to their emotional responses to the circumstances in which they find themselves. One's emotional responses will often be the cue to consider what is unique about a situation, and will link us to our previous knowledge and experience. This, in turn, will guide the application of knowledge to practice. Put simply, the fluidity of a social worker's professional identity requires self-knowledge and a constant engagement with reflection and learning.

Professionalism, social work, and emotions

In the next section, I will propose a model that locates emotions within the profession of social work. It may be useful at this stage to lay the foundations for this model. Ingram (2013a) asked social workers from across a diverse range of statutory social work contexts about their views of emotions and social work. A key finding from the study was the difficulty that many social workers had in terms of seeing the emotional content of their practice as congruent with 'being professional'. It wasn't that many respondents thought no emotions were at play within their practice but simply that they needed to be removed or marginalized to fit with professionalism. It was interesting that, despite this, the respondents found it very difficult to articulate 'how' such emotions could be removed and given what we know about the central role of emotions in human life, that is hardly surprising. Pizarro (2000) notes that although emotions are subjective in nature, they are equally rooted in experience and reality. Thus, they represent an important stream of information to guide professional decision-making (Munro, 2011).

Ruch (2012) is explicit in her quest to place emotions within the professional construct of social work. Her argument is that the 'simple' aspects of social work such as forming relationships with people in crisis are of course far from simple and require emotional intelligence and attunement. Indeed, Ruch suggests that this requirement to form relationships in complex circumstances is part of the uniqueness of the profession and as such a key facet of it. Cornish (2011) reinforces this view by noting that a key aspect of the profession of social work is the uncertainty of many of the circumstances social workers encounter. This is the antithesis of the rational and predictable aspects of some commonly held visions of what professionalism is. Cornish argues that in many ways the ability to work through a period of 'not knowing' is a key aspect of the profession and that the profession cannot be simply measured by 'the right answers' or the 'correct response'. Ferguson (2010) highlights that this complex aspect to the profession is often played out alone in environments that are threatening, menacing or intimidating. This further underlines the need for reflection and support to engage with the emotional responses and meanings that we experience in these contexts (College of Social Work, 2012; Gant et al., 2014). To think of the profession as being detached from emotions in light of this seems somewhat absurd.

If we think back to the case study, it is clear that Lorna will be full of anticipation for the challenges that lie ahead. By definition, she will be experiencing new and challenging circumstances on a daily basis as a newly qualified worker. Howe (2008) suggests that social workers are filled with emotional responses emanating both from within and from others on a daily basis. Lorna will be no different, yet she will also likely want to show that she 'knows what she is doing' as a newly qualified professional social worker. This takes us back to the ideas at the beginning this chapter about professionalism being associated with expertise and high standards. It will take time and support before Lorna feels she 'knows' how to respond to situations (Cornish, 2011) and reaches the point where any uncertainty (and the associated emotions) are seen a crucial source of information and motivation. Given the coverage in the media about apparent poor judgement on the part of a fellow practitioner in her field, it is likely that the temptation to avoid blurriness and uncertainty is increased. Ferguson (2005) notes that such avoidance can lead to dysfunctional decision-making rather than safer decision-making.

Voices of practitioners

Janet, a children and families social worker

'I think you have to be able to display empathy within practice but your own emotions should not be apparent within practice, as this could compromise your professionalism.'

It would seem that there is something odd about empathy being coupled with the removal of emotions, but in Janet's terms, this is not a tension but a professional necessity. The idea that one's professionalism can be compromised by the role of emotions seems to suggest that there is a construct of the profession that is technically rational in nature.

Fiona, a learning disabilities care manager

'While I would not allow my feelings to rule my practice, I do not wish to be the type of social worker where I am "unfeeling", and want to be a caring professional. I do

not want to feel detached from the service users I am working with, and believe that empathy and a caring attitude can go a long way in this job.'

Fiona stakes a claim for emotions and feelings having a central role in establishing the social worker/service user relationship, and uses the familiar but significant phrase 'caring professional'. By adding the suffix 'al' to the word profession, the debate about the role of emotions becomes more manageable and less incongruous.

Emotions and social work: a professional model

This chapter has explored the role of emotions within the context of the social work profession. The focus on the word 'professional' emerged from the findings of Ingram (2013a), as it was common for social workers to use the word professional to explain the inappropriateness of using emotions within practice or at least identify it as being an area of tension and complexity. The notion of being a professional is often underpinned by technical-rational constructs where certainty and tangible outcomes are highly valued (Brodie et al., 2008). When professionalism is viewed through this lens, it is natural and understandable that workers find it difficult to express how or if emotions impact on their practice. This is further underpinned by confusing and contradictory messages from policy and literature about what the profession of social work entails.

The model presented here is intended to provide readers with a framework to encourage and support them to acknowledge the place of emotions within their practice, and to recognize that this is echoed throughout current narratives about the profession. It pulls together the key themes of this book into what it is hoped is a usable model that will not only clarify the thinking presented here but also provide momentum for promoting the place of emotions more generally within social practice.

The discussion in this chapter has brought together a range of themes that contribute to an image of a profession where emotions should, and do, have a significant role. So often this type of discussion can edge towards an unhelpful separation of potential models, such as highlighting a technical-rational model *or* a relationship-based model. The themes and topics explored throughout this book suggest that the separation is neither helpful nor realistic. It has already been argued that emotions and rational thought are usefully and inextricably connected. Indeed, regardless of the processes and knowledge brought to bear on social work practice, it is the ability to form positive relationships and partnerships with service users that is at the core of the activity. Hennessey (2011: 17) underlines this when he states: 'we should see social work as a distinctive profession where separating oneself from one's emotions is tantamount to separating oneself from the client'. This statement was made in the context of a relationship-based view of practice and resonates strongly with current visions and aspirations of the profession (Munro, 2011).

It is evident that there are often real or perceived boundaries between the practice of the individual social worker, the organizational messages about the profession, and national policy and guidance. The key strands that contribute to the realization of a construct of the profession of social work are shown in Figure 8.1. Clearly, there is a great deal of detail and further factors involved, but the aim of this diagram is to suggest that these strands often sit beside rather than are connected to each other. This leads to the contested nature of the profession and the uncertainty and disjuncture that this gives rise to, as discussed in the preceding chapters. The separation reinforces the sense that these strands can appear at odds with each other, or at the very least are open to a range of emphases and interpretations. It is clear that these differences in interpretation and experience can arise within team and supervisory relationships. It is heartening to see that the messages from the Social Work Task Force (DCSF, 2009) regarding the enhancement of the reflective aspects of social work, and the messages from the Munro Report (Munro, 2011) regarding greater autonomy and recognition of the emotional aspects of practice, appear to overlap and chime with each other. It is the operationalization and cascading down of these messages that are the crucial aspect of this if the three circles in Figure 8.1 are to merge meaningfully.

Figure 8.1 Facets of the profession

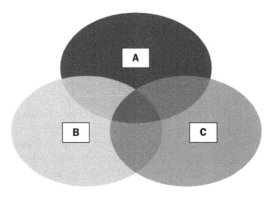

Figure 8.2 Relationship between the facets of the profession

The intersection between the three circles in Figure 8.2 is crucial to considering the role of emotions in social work practice. It is the area where the congruent messages about the role of emotions from across the profession come together. By this I mean the place where the aforementioned polarized strands can cohabit within a single construct of the profession. This book has highlighted the ethical, sociological, political, and psychological elements that contribute to the intertwining of emotions and social work practice. I will use that intersection as the foundation of a construct of the profession that integrates the emotional elements of practice within it, rather than from outside it.

The model below is intended to locate the social work professional within a complex system of influences with the explicit intention of illustrating the valuable contribution of these influences rather than perpetuating the unhelpful divisions noted above. The focus of this book and the model below is on locating the role of emotions within the social work profession and practice. The conceptual framework of emotions proposed in Chapter 1 underlines the inescapable role that emotions play in the reality of practice and indeed human experience. What was heartening and intuitive when constructing this model was that the overlaps between the quadrants were identifiable, realistic, and appropriate. The model is based on four key areas of influence. These are:

- Organizational culture
- Social work practice
- Supervision, support, and reflection
- Professional frameworks, policy, and legislation.

The individual social work professional is placed at the centre of the model with each quadrant explicitly linked to the others in an interdependent process (see Figure 8.3).

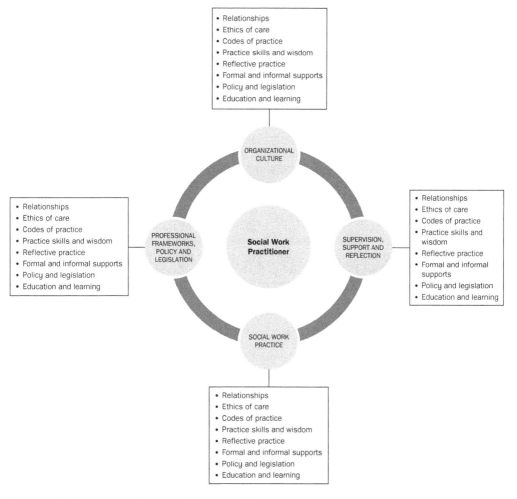

Figure 8.3 Embedding emotions in social work model

This is a crucial aspect of the model, in that the quadrants are developed to enhance clarity rather than to perpetuate the boundaries between them. I have then built the model outwards to identify what I believe to be the key components of each quadrant. As noted above, the key components have a resonance across all four quadrants, which have emerged throughout the chapters of this book and which I believe to be a valuable contribution to developing a model that locates emotions within it rather than on the periphery. I will provide a commentary to accompany the model and reflect on the process of its construction.

Let us begin by taking each quadrant in turn and discuss the elements within each. I will then discuss the relationships between the quadrants and how this interdependent relationship creates a dynamic and flexible construct for the profession.

1. Organizational culture

It was clear from the discussion in Chapter 7 that organizational culture has a direct impact on the perceived appropriateness of articulating, recording, and using emotions in social work practice. The notion of a 'learning culture' is intended to create a space for the value placed on reflection, autonomy, and enhancement of practice. Within that construct there should be room for social workers to explore the emotional elements of their practice. By allowing a culture of 'safety' for this to take place, workers will feel able to exercise their emotional intelligence by identifying, managing, and using their emotions in practice. This is directly related to adapting the norms and rules that have influenced and encouraged the marginalization of emotions.

This culture of openness and safety in a sense reflects key social work values and qualities required within a relationship between social worker and service user. The congruence between organizational culture and direct practice is a crucial aspect of this. As identified earlier in this chapter, there are policy documents, professional frameworks, and legislation that underpin an ethos that values the social work relationship, transparency, and increasing autonomy. This should contribute to an organizational sense of the appropriateness of such an approach, while also helpfully locating such messages alongside other key aspects of policy that emphasize, for example, the importance of procedures and evidence bases. Once organizations develop the ability to see the congruence between existing professional frameworks and the role of emotions and relationships within practice, it is possible to envisage there being an explicit and implicit impact on the nature of how social work practice is written and recorded in informal and formal settings.

I have identified the presentational aspects of practice/emotions and noted the impact of the rules and norms of organizations. The increased congruence between organizational culture and practice reality will *still* provide a socially constructed backdrop for how workers feel they should present themselves, but the nature of this presentation will shift towards greater openness and reflection. This brings us back to the notion of a healthy learning organization, which, when underpinned by the ethics of care, can manage the uncertain and 'risky' elements of practice by acknowledging and claiming the social work relationship as a central driver within the culture.

2. Social work practice

This book has repeatedly highlighted the place and importance of relationships and how this is often pitted against rational-technical visions of the profession. What is undeniable is that these relationships are seen as central to the activity of being a social worker and as such the links between 'being professional' and these relationships is cogent. It is important to note that the wider frameworks and policy that underpin the organizational culture are directly linked to the individual worker also. The requirement for professional registration has underlined the explicit relationship between individual social workers and the professional codes and frameworks that they agree to adhere to. Taking this regulatory influence as a starting point, social workers can acknowledge the messages about the centrality of relationships with service users as well as expectations about autonomy and reflection. This fits well with the inter-personal aspects of emotions contained within the conceptual framework. When there is greater congruency of organizational messages, then the dramaturgical elements of professional presentation can more easily accommodate this emphasis. If we then link this to our discussion about the ethics of care in Chapter 6, we can create an ethical space for social workers to locate the importance of their relationships with service users.

The model underlines the importance for social workers to develop their ability to manage the emotional elements of these relationships and use them to establish open and empathic communication. This we know to be highly valued by service users and reflected in the codes of practice, and as such the rules and norms in which social workers operate should facilitate this. It is clear that the relationships between social workers and service users are subject to professional boundaries and roles that may contribute to a sense of uncertainty about how emotions fit comfortably with 'being professional'. By harnessing the messages noted above about the profession and encouraging the role of emotions within practice, social workers can make comfortable links between professional frameworks and their practice. By this I mean that the explicit use and acknowledgement of the emotional awareness, management, and attunement elements of emotional intelligence can provide a bridge between the frameworks and the reality of practice by countering the previously intangible aspects of emotions.

A key to establishing a view of practice that values the emotions and the centrality of the social work relationship is the congruence between organizational and national messages about individual autonomy, responsibility, and expertise. It is envisaged that this vision of a social work professional will be cultivated through the aforementioned learning culture and also be underpinned by the regulatory requirement for continued professional development. This is crucial in terms of giving all parties involved the confidence that greater autonomy and relationship-based approaches are underpinned by a vigorous and explicit requirement for reflection and learning. This provides a rigour to the place of emotions and relationships, and in so doing, the more technicist areas of practice, such as risk assessment, may be integrated more comfortably.

3. Supervision, support, and reflection

There are very clear connections between the organizational culture and the messages that social workers receive about exploring the emotional aspects of their practice in supervision. It is also clear from Chapter 6 that regardless of wider organizational messages, there is scope for supervisors to vary their interpretation about what supervision involves. It is anticipated that the connectedness of national, organizational, and individual professional constructs within this model will mitigate against a lack of congruence and consistency between supervisors. An example of this interconnectedness across levels is the notion of role-modelling – in this case, it is about the organization, supervisor, and social worker all exhibiting an awareness and value about the emotional and relationship aspects of practice. This ties in well with the notion of social consensus suggested by Rosenberg (1990) and the influence this has on emotional expression and understandings. If this flows from a core cultural ethos, then it would be incongruous for supervision to sideline these aspects in favour of managerialist and outcome-focused approaches. This clearly links back to the discussion of the socially constructed elements of emotions in practice. There is a strong case to be made for supervisors being able to provide a role-modelling approach involving openness, genuineness, and emotional intelligence. This may provide a useful link between management and practice experience/wisdom and move away from a line management-orientated approach.

Chapter 6 noted the important role of informal support from colleagues and peers. In its purest form, this would likely continue to exist within any cultural ethos. However, given a culture where the emotional aspects of practice are valued, used, and explored, the need for such support may diminish. It would, however, be a mistake to be complacent about informal types of support. The benefits of shared expertise, the immediacy of support, and the opportunity for reflection would remain attractive and relevant aspects of informal support. Indeed, given a shift in culture, this may be encouraged through the confidence of social workers to access the support and advice that meet their needs. The establishment of physical spaces and semi-structured opportunities for peer support would further develop this important theme. Linked to this discussion is the idea of peer mentoring schemes, which represent a quasi-informal approach to linking peers together. Again, this would not need to be subject to the issue of 'feeling safe' if the culture of the organization at all levels explicitly valued the emotional and complex aspects of the relationships with service users. I noted in the previous two quadrants the congruent messages enshrined in professional codes and polices – this should provide a reassuring context for supervision and other supportive systems to embrace these elements rather than be used to marginalize them.

4. Professional frameworks, policy and legislation

The discussion regarding the preceding three quadrants covers much of the ground on the compatibility and importance of national guidelines and frameworks. In this book, we have seen examples of where these documents can be used to promote or marginalize the emotional aspects of practice. Within this model, it is intended that they set the foundation for a dynamic and evolving culture where the relationship-based aspirations can interact positively with the technicist requirements of practice. This is about a cultural shift organizationally and individually as much as it is about the documents themselves. It is clear that the messages that support the role of emotions and relationships in practice are to be found across the key professional documents, so it is this cultural shift 'on the ground' that needs to turn these messages from being contested aspirations to accepted elements of a professional construct.

The presence of social work education at pre- and post-qualifying stages within this quadrant is crucial. The place of emotions and relationships within practice is evident across the curricula of social work training and enshrined within the professional standards required at qualifying and post-qualifying levels. This is an essential element of this model, as it reflects its cyclical nature and that each of the elements should and must feed into each other.

The discussion above highlights the key elements of each quadrant. I chose a model that was fluid and dynamic and emphasized the connectedness of the key elements. It was heartening that the connectedness between these elements was not difficult to ascertain, and the content of this book has helped to shine light on the areas where social workers find the role of emotions most difficult to articulate and express, and those areas where they see congruence or the potential for it.

During the development of this model, many prototypes were rejected. One of the themes that recur throughout this book is the 'balance' between apparently competing factors. For example, the balance between the relationship-based aspects of practice and technical–rational aspects. I tried to develop a model that used the metaphor of balance in the form of scales. The strength of this approach was that it accommodated and recognized that apparently opposing elements could be used in combination. The key weakness of this approach was that to only weigh up different factors fell short of removing the boundaries between them. Instead, it perpetuates the sense that they co-exist but in an uncomfortable manner. This would in turn fall short of the cultural shift required and potentially leave these strands as contested and open to defensive or narrow interpretation.

This chapter has in many ways brought us back to the beginning in the sense that it has emphasized that the role of emotions has an important role in the role, function, and actions of social workers. What this chapter seeks to add to our discussion is a model that places emotions at the heart of what is to be a social work professional rather than at the periphery. And this model is based on existing knowledge, professional narratives, and social workers' views. In a sense, it simply sheds light on what is already present but which struggles to be seen due to competing and often irreconcilable perspectives.

Key learning points

- The concept of a 'profession' carries a range of informal cultural assumptions that impact upon how social work is viewed internally and externally.
- The notion of professional identity was proposed. It is a 'self-concept' and one that is developed through a range of factors including experiences, frameworks, emotions, context, policy, and culture.
- A professional model was developed with emotions at its core. It draws from existing knowledge of the profession and as such provides a useful and powerful illustration of how emotions are not incongruent with 'being professional'.

Further reading

College of Social Work (2012) *Professional Capabilities Framework* [http://www.tcsw.org.uk/pcf.aspx].
This has been referred to throughout this book and provides a clear framework to locate discussions about the place of emotions within the profession.

Cree, V. (2003) *Becoming a Social Worker*. London: Routledge.
This book offers a series of accounts relating to the motivations and experiences of becoming a social worker. It provides an interesting backdrop to any discussion about what social work is and means.

Concluding thoughts

Chapter 8 pulled together the key themes that emerged from my exploration of the concept of emotions and the powerful role that it has within social work practice. The conceptual framework introduced in Chapter 1 underlines the fact that emotions are unquestionably a key mechanism through which human beings make sense of the world and determine their responses and behaviours. It was noted that emotions have roots in our previous experiences (conscious and unconscious) and are framed and moulded by prevailing cultural cues and norms. The proliferation of data emerging from neuroscience research confirms the central role of brain function and emotional processes, and provides a robust and tangible evidence base to what can often seem a rather slippery and diffuse concept. The key conclusion that one draws from any given contextual analysis of emotions is that they exist and they are immensely powerful and important in our lives and relationships. This is the key foundation stone of this book, as it provided the core driver behind my interest in this topic: *if emotions are so significant to the lives of humans, then by association emotions will have a pivotal role in the work of social workers.* It may appear a rather simple foundation, but it is one (as we have seen in this book) that is both contested and complex.

It has been shown that emotions in social work operate on many levels. We examined a range of practice scenarios to highlight the significant emotional responses that social workers may have to their practice. This is in part due to the often complex and fluid nature of the lives of the service users with whom they form professional relationships, but also their own emotional experiences and thresholds, which lead them to appraise situations in a unique way. Critical reflection was seen to be an essential activity for social workers to engage in if their emotional responses to practice are to be acknowledged, understood, and used effectively. Without the development of such reflective skills and abilities (emotional intelligence is a useful concept here), the influence of our emotions may remain unknown and unmanaged. By ignoring and marginalizing emotions in thought and discourse, we do not reduce their presence or influence, rather we miss crucial opportunities to shed light on the emotional worlds of ourselves and others and in turn make sense of the blurred and complex situations we find ourselves in. Without an awareness and knowledge of our emotions, we simply are not able to meaningfully engage in empathetic and attuned relationships with service users.

This book is aimed at students, social work practitioners (at all levels), and organizations, as there is interplay between the individual and their professional role and context. It is hoped the activities and messages in this book will act as a catalyst at an individual, organizational, and professional level to develop the processes, language, permissions, and culture required to raise the profile of emotion in social work practice. I have highlighted a range of sources where one can seek reassurances about the place of emotions in the social work profession, such as the Professional Capabilities Framework (College of Social Work, 2012). However, there remains a gap between the implicit messages of such professional narratives and the reality of the experiences of social workers who may find themselves in professional cultures where an increasing rational-technical conception of practice prevails. This book has argued that there is a balance to be struck here rather than a case of 'either/or'. The next step for the social work profession is to continue to debate and reflect upon this tension. It is hoped this book will help to achieve this balance with clarity and certainty, since emotions have a huge role to play in our lives both as social workers and human beings.

References

Agass, D. (2002) Countertransference, supervision and the reflection process, *Journal of Social Work Practice*, 16 (2): 125–33.

Aldridge, M. (1996) Dragged to market: being a profession in the postmodern world, *British Journal of Social Work*, 26 (2): 177–94.

Arthur, M.B. (2008) Examining contemporary careers: a call for interdisciplinary inquiry, *Human Relations*, 61 (2): 163–86.

Ash, S. and Clayton, P. (2004) The articulated learning: an approach to guided reflection and assessment, *Innovative Higher Education*, 29 (2): 137–54.

Ayre, P. (2001) Notes from child protection and the media: lessons from the last three decades, *British Journal of Social Work*, 31 (6): 887–901.

Bailey, R. and Brake M. (1976) *Radical Social Work*. New York: Pantheon.

Bamford, T. (1982) *Managing Social Work*. London: Tavistock.

Barrett, L. (2012) Emotions are real, *Emotion*, 12 (3): 413–29.

Barsky, A. (2009) *Ethics and Values in Social Work*. Oxford: Oxford University Press.

Bassot, B. (2013) *The Reflective Journal*. Basingstoke: Palgrave Macmillan.

Beckett, C. and Maynard, A. (2013) *Values and Ethics in Social Work*. Basingstoke: Palgrave Macmillan.

Beddoe, L. (2010) Surveillance or reflection: professional supervision in a risk society, *British Journal of Social Work*, 40 (4): 1279–96.

Biesteck, F. (1957) *The Casework Relationship*. London: Allen & Unwin.

Bion, W. (1962) *Learning from Experience*. London: Tavistock.

Bogo, M. and McKnight, K. (2006) Clinical supervision in social work: a review of the research literature, *Clinical Supervisor*, 24 (1): 49–67.

Bolton, S. (2000) Who cares? Offering emotions work as a 'gift' in the nursing labour process, *Journal of Advanced Nursing*, 32 (3): 580–6.

Bolton, S. and Boyd, C. (2003) Trolley dolly or skilled emotion manager? Moving on from Hochschild's *Managed Heart*, Work, Employment and Society, 17 (2): 289–308.

Bower, M. (2005) Psychoanalytic theories for social work practice, in M. Bower (ed.) *Psychoanalytic Theory for Social Work: Thinking under fire*. London: Routledge.

Bracket, M., Palomera, R., Mosja-Kaja, J., Reyes, M. and Salovey, P. (2010) Emotion-regulation ability, burnout and job satisfaction among British secondary school teachers, *Psychology in the Schools*, 47 (4): 406–17.

British Association of Social Workers (BASW) (2012a) *Social Media Policy*. Birmingham: BASW.

British Association of Social Workers (BASW) (2012b) *The Code of Ethics for Social Work: Statement of principles*. Birmingham: BASW.

Brodie, I., Nottingham, C. and Plunkett, S. (2008) A tale of two reports: social work in Scotland from *Social Work and the Community* (1966) to *Changing Lives* (2006), *British Journal of Social Work*, 38 (4): 697–715.

Bronstein, L. (2003) A model for interdisciplinary collaboration, *Social Work*, 48 (3): 297–306.

Cadman, C. and Brewer, J. (2001) Emotional intelligence: a vital pre-requisite for recruitment in nursing, *Journal of Nursing Management*, 9 (6): 321–4.

Care Council for Wales (CCW) (2004) *Code of Practice: Standards for social care workers and their managers* [http://www.ccwales.org.uk].

Clore, G. and Ortony, A. (2000) Cognition in emotion: always sometimes or never?, in R. Lane and L. Nadel (eds.) *Cognitive Neuroscience of Emotions*. New York: Oxford University Press.

College of Social Work (2012) *Professional Capabilities Framework* [http://www.tcsw.org.uk/pcf.aspx].

Collins, E. and Daley, E. (2011) *Decision-making and Social Work in Scotland: The role of evidence and practice wisdom*. Glasgow: IRISS.

Collins, S. (2007) Social workers, resilience, positive emotions and optimism, *Practice*, 19 (4): 255–69.

Cornish, S. (2011) Negative capability and social work: insights from Keats, Bion and business, *Journal of Social Work Practice*, 25 (2): 135–48.

Coulshed, V. and Orme, J. (2006) *Social Work Practice* (4th edn.). Basingstoke: Palgrave Macmillan.

Crisp, B.R., Green Lister, P. and Dutton, K. (2005) Integrated Assessment: New assessment methods. Evaluation of an innovative method of assessment: critical incident analysis. Working Paper. Glasgow: Scottish Institute for Excellence in Social Work Education [http://www.iriss.org.uk/sites/default/files/sieswe-nam-evaluation-critical-incident-analysis-2005-02.pdf].

Crossan, M., Lane, H. and White, R. (1999) An organizational learning framework, *Academic Management Review*, 24 (3): 522–37.

Currer, C. (2007) *Loss and Social Work*. Exeter: Learning Matters.

Damasio, A. (1994) *Descartes' Error: Emotion, reason and the human brain*. New York: Putnam.

Damasio, A. (2000) A second chance for emotions, in R. Lane and L. Nadel (eds.) *Cognitive Neuroscience of Emotions*. New York: Oxford University Press.

Damasio, A., Tranel, D. and Damasio, H. ([1991] 1998) Somatic markers and the guidance of behaviours, in J. Jenkins, K. Oatley and N. Stein (eds.) *Human Emotions: A reader*. Oxford: Blackwell.

Darwin, C. ([1890] 1998) The expression of emotions in man and animals. in J. Jenkins, K. Oatley and N. Stein (eds.) *Human Emotions: A reader*. Oxford: Blackwell.

Data Protection Act (1998) [http://www.legislation.gov.uk/all?title=Data%20Protection%20Act%201998].

Davidson, R. (1994) On emotion, mood and related affective constructs, in P. Ekman and R. Davidson (eds.) *The Nature of Emotion: Fundamental questions*. New York: Oxford University Press.

Davies, H. and Kinloch, H. (2000) Critical incident analysis: facilitating reflection and transfer of learning, in V.E. Cree and C. Macauley (eds.) *Transfer of Learning in Professional and Vocational Education*. London: Routledge.

D'Cruz, H., Gillingham, P. and Melendez, S. (2007) Reflexivity: a concept and its meanings for practitioners working with children and families, *British Journal of Social Work*, 37 (1): 73–90.

Department for Children Schools and Families (DCSF) (2009) *Building a Safe, Confident Future: The final report of the Social Work Task Force*. London: DCSF.

Doel, M. (2006) *Using Groupwork*. London: Routledge.

Doel, M. (2009) *Social Work Placements: A traveller's guide*. London: Routledge.

Doel, M. and Kelly, T. (2013) *A–Z of Groups and Groupwork*. Basingstoke: Palgrave Macmillan.

Dominelli, L. (2009) *Introducing Social Work*. Cambridge: Polity Press.

Donnellan, H. and Jack, G. (2010) *The Survival Guide for Newly Qualified Child and Family Social Workers: Hitting the ground running*. London. Jessica Kingsley.

Dow, J. (2008) Our journey: perspectives from people who use services, in M. McPhail (ed.) *Service User and Carer Involvement: Beyond good intentions*. Edinburgh: Dunedin Academic.

Dowson, E., Gee, M., Ingram, R., Leeson, B. and Mackenzie, G. (2010) Service user, carer, practice educator and academic partnership in evaluating decision making of social work students, in H. Burgess and J. Carpenter (eds.) *The Outcome of Social Work Education: Developing Evaluation Methods*. London: SWAP.

Egan, G. (2010) *The Skilled Helper* (9th edn.). Belmont, CA: Brookes/Cole.

Ekman, P. (1977) Biological and cultural contributions to body and facial movement, in J. Blackin (ed.) *The Anthropology of the Body*. London: Academic Press.

Ekman, P. (1989) The argument and evidence about universals in facial expressions of emotions, in H. Wagner and A. Manstead (eds.) *Handbook of Social Psychophysiology*. Chichester: Wiley.

Ekman, P. and Friesen, W. (1971) Constants across culture in the face and emotion, *Journal of Personality and Social Psychology*, 17 (2): 124–9.

England, H. (1986) *Social Work as Art*. London: Allen & Unwin.

Fenton, J. (2012) Bringing together messages from the literature on criminal justice social work and disjuncture: the importance of helping, *British Journal of Social Work*, 42 (5): 941–56.

Ferguson, H. (2003) Outline of a critical best practice approach to social work and social care, *British Journal of Social Work*, 33 (8): 1005–24.

Ferguson, H. (2005) Working with violence, the emotions and the psycho-social dynamics of child protection: reflections on the Victoria Climbié case. *Social Work Education*, 24 (7): 781–95.

Ferguson, H. (2010) Walks, home visits and atmospheres: risks and the everyday practices and mobilities of social work and child protection, *British Journal of Social Work*, 40 (4): 1100–17.

Fook, J. and Gardner, F. (2007) *Practising Critical Reflection*. Maidenhead: Open University Press.

Forgas, J. (2001) *Handbook of Affect and Social Cognition*. New York: Guilford Press.

Fredrickson, B. (1998) What good are positive emotions?, *Review of General Psychology*, 2 (3): 300–19.

Freud, S. (1959) *Inhibitions, Symptoms, Anxiety*. New York: Norton.

Fridja, N. (1988) The laws of emotions, *American Psychologist*, 43 (5): 349–58.

Frost, N., Robinson, M. and Anning, A. (2005) Social workers in multidisciplinary teams: issues and dilemmas for professional practice, *Child and Family Social Work*, 10 (3): 187–96.

Gant, L., Kinman, G. and Alexander, K. (2014) What's all this talk about emotion? Developing emotional intelligence in social work students, *Social Work Education*, 33 (7): 874–89.

Gee, M. and McPhail, M. (2008) The voice of service users and carers in universities, in M. McPhail (ed.) *Service User and Carer Involvement: Beyond good intentions*. Edinburgh: Dunedin Academic.

General Social Care Council (GSCC) (2004) *Codes of Practice for Social Care Workers and Employers*. London: GSCC.

Gibbs, G. (1988) *Learning by Doing: A guide to teaching and learning methods*. Oxford: Oxford Brookes University.

Gibelman, M. and Schervish, P. (1997) Supervision in social work: characteristics and trends in a changing environment, *Clinical Supervisor*, 16 (2): 1–16.

Glassman, P. and Hadad, M. (2013) *Approaches to Psychology* (6th edn.). Maidenhead: Open University Press.

Goffman, E. (1983) The interaction order, *American Sociological Review*, 48 (1): 1–17.

Goleman, D. (1995) *Emotional Intelligence*. London: Bloomsbury.

Gould, N. and Baldwin, M. (2004) *Social Work, Critical Reflection and the Learning Organisation*. Aldershot: Ashgate.

Grant, L., Kinman, G. and Baker, S. (2014) *Emotional Resilience in the Social Work Curriculum: A research report*. York: HEA.

Hafford-Letchfield, T. (2009) *Management and Organisations in Social Work*. Exeter: Learning Matters.

Halr, H. (2012) The purpose and duration of supervision, and the training and discipline of supervisors: what social workers say they need to provide effective services, *British Journal of Social Work*, 43 (8): 1562–88.

Hall, C., Slembrouck, S. and Sarangi, S. (2006) *Language Practices in Social Work: Categorisation and accountability in child welfare*. London: Routledge.

Hannah, E.F.S., Ingram, R., Kerr, C. and Kelly, T.B. (2014) Inquiry-based learning for interprofessional education, in P. Blessinger and J.M. Carfora (eds.) *Inquiry-Based Learning for the Arts, Humanities and Social Sciences: A conceptual and practical resource for educators*. Innovations in Higher Education Teaching and Learning, Vol. 2. Bingley, UK: Emerald Group.

Harding, T. and Beresford, P. (1995) *The Standards We Expect: What service users and carers want from social workers*. London: National Institute of Social Work.

Hawkins, P. and Shohet, R. (2006) *Supervision in the Helping Professions* (3rd edn.). Buckingham: Open University Press.

Healy, K. and Mulholland, J. (2012) *Writing Skills for Social Workers*. London: Sage.

Hennessey, R. (2011) *Relationship Skills in Social Work*. London: Sage.

Hochschild, A.R. (1983) *The Managed Heart: Commercialization of human feeling*. Los Angeles, CA: University of California Press.

Holland, S. (1999) Discourses of decision making in child protection: conducting comprehensive assessments in Britain, *International Journal of Social Welfare*, 8 (4): 276–86.

Holmes, M. (2010) The emotionalization of reflexivity, *Sociology*, 44 (1): 139–54.

Houston, S. (2012) Engaging with the crooked timber of humanity: value pluralism and social work, *British Journal of Social Work*, 42 (4): 652–68.

Howe, D. (1993) *On Being a Client: Understanding the process of counselling and psychotherapy*. London: Sage.

Howe, D. (2008) *The Emotionally Intelligent Social Worker*. Basingstoke: Palgrave Macmillan.

Howe, D. (2013) *Empathy: What it is and why it matters*. Basingstoke: Palgrave Macmillan.

Huuskonen, S. and Vakkari, P. (2013) 'I did it my way': social workers as secondary designers of client information system, *Information Process Management*, 49 (1): 380–91.

Ibarra, H. (1999) Provisional selves: experimenting with image and identity in professional adaptation, *Administrative Science Quarterly*, 44 (4): 764–91.

Ingram, R. (2013a) Emotions and social work practice, unpublished PhD thesis, University of Dundee.

Ingram, R. (2013b) Emotions, social work practice and supervision: an uneasy alliance?, *Journal of Social Work Practice*, 27 (1): 5–19.

Ingram, R. (2013c) Exploring emotions within formal and informal forums: messages from social work practitioners, *British Journal of Social Work* [DOI: doi: 10.1093/bjsw/bct166].

Ingram, R. (2013d) Locating emotional intelligence at the heart of social work practice, *British Journal of Social Work*, 43 (5): 987–1004.

Ingram, R., Fenton, J., Hodson, A. and Jindal-Snape, D. (2014) *Reflective Social Work Practice*. Basingstoke: Palgrave Macmillan.

Isen, A., Daubman, K. and Nowicki, G. ([1987] 1998) Positive affect facilitates creative problem solving, in J. Jenkins, K. Oatley and N. Stein (eds.) *Human Emotions: A reader*. Oxford: Blackwell.

James, W. ([1890] 1998) The principles of psychology, in J. Jenkins, K. Oatley and N. Stein (eds.) *Human Emotions: A reader*. Oxford: Blackwell.

Jankowiak, W. and Fischer, E. ([1992] 1998) A cross cultural perspective on romantic love, in J. Jenkins, K. Oatley and N. Stein (eds.) *Human Emotions: A reader*. Oxford: Blackwell.

Jenkins, J., Oatley, K. and Stein, N. (1998) History and culture, in J. Jenkins, K. Oatley and N. Stein (eds.) *Human Emotions: A reader*. Oxford: Blackwell.

Jindal-Snape, D. and Ingram, R. (2013) Understanding and supporting triple transitions of international doctoral students: ELT and SuReCom models, *Journal of Perspectives in Applied Academic Practice*, 1 (1): 17–24.

John, M. and Trevithick, P. (2012) Psychodynamic thinking in social work practice, in P. Stepney and D. Ford (eds.) *Social Work Models, Methods and Theories*. Lyme Regis: Russell House.

Johns, C. (1994) Nuances of reflection, *Journal of Clinical Nursing*, 3 (2): 71–5.

Jones, C. (2001) Voices from the front line: state social workers and new Labour, *British Journal of Social Work*, 31 (4): 547–62.

Kadushin, A. (1985) *Supervision in Social Work* (2nd edn.). New York: Columbia University Press.

Kant, I. (1785) *Groundwork of the Metaphysic of Morals*, New York: Harper & Row.

Keinemans, S. (2014) Be sensible: emotions in social work ethics and Education, *British Journal of Social Work* [DOI: 10.1093/bjsw/bcu057].

Kennedy-Moore, E. and Watson, J. (1999) *Expressing Emotions: Myths, realities and therapeutic strategies*. London: Guilford Press.

Kerka, S. (1995) The learning organization: myths and realities, *Eric Clearinghouse* [http://www.cete.org/acve/docgen.asp?tbl=archive&ID=A028].

Kinman, G. and Grant, L. (2011) Exploring stress resilience in trainee social workers: the role of emotional and social competencies, *British Journal of Social Work*, 41 (2): 261–75.

Kolb, D. (1984) *Experiential Learning: Experience as a source of learning and development*. Englewood Cliffs, NJ: Prentice-Hall.

Koprowska, J. (2005) *Communication and Interpersonal Skills in Social Work*. Exeter: Learning Matters.

Lane, R. and Nadel, L. (2000) Preface, in R. Lane and L. Nadel (eds.) *Cognitive Neuroscience of Emotions*. New York: Oxford University Press.

Lane, R., Nadel, L., Allen, J. and Kaszniak, A. (2000) The study of emotions from the perspective of cognitive neuroscience, in R. Lane and L. Nadel (eds.) *Cognitive Neuroscience of Emotions*. New York: Oxford University Press.

Lay, K. and McGuire, L. (2010) Building a lens for critical reflection and reflexivity in social work education, *Social Work Education*, 29 (5): 539–50.

Lazarus, R. ([1991] 1998) Emotion and adaptation, in J. Jenkins, K. Oatley and N. Stein (eds.) *Human Emotions: A reader*. Oxford: Blackwell.

Lazarus, R. and Lazarus, B. (1994) *Passion and Reason*. New York: Oxford University Press.

LeDoux, J. (1993) Emotional memory systems in the brain, *Behavioural and Brain Research*, 58 (1): 66–79.

LeDoux, J. (1997) *The Emotional Brain: The mysterious underpinnings of emotional life*. New York: Simon & Schuster.

Lindebaum, D. and Cartwright, S. (2011) Leadership effectiveness: the costs and benefits of being emotionally intelligent, *Leadership and Organization Development Journal*, 32 (3): 281–90.

Lishman, J. (2009) *Communication in Social Work* (2nd edn.). Basingstoke: Palgrave Macmillan.

Lomax, R., Jones, K., Leigh, S. and Gay, C. (2010) *Surviving Your Social Work Placement*. Basingstoke: Palgrave Macmillan.

Mann, S. (2004) People work: emotion management, stress and coping, *British Journal of Guidance and Counselling*, 32 (2): 205–21.

Marsick, V.J. *and* Watkins, K.E. (1990) *Informal and Incidental Learning in the Workplace*. London: Routledge.

Maslach, C. (1979) Negative emotional biasing of unexplained arousal, *Journal of Personality and Social Psychology*, 37 (6): 953–69.

Mayer, J. and Cobb, C. (2000) Educational policy on emotional intelligence: does it make sense?, *Educational Psychology Review*, 12 (2): 163–83.

Mayer, J. and Timms, N. (1970) *The Client Speaks: Working-class impressions of casework*. London: Routledge.

Mayer, J.D., DiPaolo, M.T. and Salovey, P. (1990) Perceiving affective content in ambiguous visual stimuli: a component of emotional intelligence, *Journal of Personality Assessment*, 54 (3/4): 772–81.

Mayer, J.D. and Salovey, P. (1997) What is emotional intelligence?, in P. Salovey and D. Sluyter (eds.) *Emotional Development and Emotional Intelligence: Education implications*. New York: Basic Books.

McGregor, D. (2006) *The Human Side of Enterprise*. New York: McGraw-Hill.

McLaughlin, H. (2009) What's in a name: 'client', 'patient', 'customer', 'consumer', 'expert by experience', 'service user' – what's next?, *British Journal of Social Work*, 39 (6): 1101–17.

McNeil, F., Batchelor, S., Burnett, R. and Knox, J. (2005) *Reducing Re-offending – Key practice skills*. Edinburgh: Scottish Executive.

Megele, C. (2012) Social care and the eprofessionalism era, *The Guardian Online* [http://www.theguardian.com/social-care-network/2012/apr/25].

Moon, J. (1999) *Reflection in Learning and Professional Development*. London: RoutledgeFalmer.

Moon, J. (2004) *A Handbook of Reflective and Experiential Learning*. London: Routledge.

Morrison, T. (2007) Emotional intelligence, emotion and social work: context, characteristics, complications and contribution, *British Journal of Social Work*, 37 (2): 245–63.

Munro, E.R. (2011) *The Munro Review of Child Protection: Final Report – A child centred system*. London: DfE [//www.bardag-lscb.co.uk/Publications/Documents/TheMunroReviewofChildProtection Final Report.pdf].

Murphy, D., Duggan, M. and Joseph, S. (2013) Relationship based social work and its compatibility with the person centred approach: principled versus instrumental perspectives, *British Journal of Social Work*, 43 (4): 703–19.

National Association of Social Workers (NASW) (2008) *Code of Ethics*. Washington, DC: NASW.

Noble, C. and Irwin, J. (2009) Social work supervision: an exploration of the current challenges in a rapidly changing social, economic and political environment, *Journal of Social Work*, 9 (3): 345–58.

Northern Ireland Social Care Council (NISSC) (2004) *Codes of Practice for Social Care Workers and Employers of Social Care Workers* [http://www.niscc.info/index.php/codes-of-practice].

O'Donoghue, K. and Tsui, M. (2011) Towards a professional supervision culture: the development of social work supervision in Aotearoa New Zealand, *International Social Work*, 55 (1): 5–28.

O'Rourke, L. (2010) *Recording in Social Work: Not just an administrative task*. Bristol: Policy Press.

O'Sullivan, T. (1999) *Decision Making in Social Work*. Basingstoke: Palgrave Macmillan.

Parker, D., Webb, J. and D'Souza, B. (1995) The value of critical incident analysis as an educational tool and its relationship to experiential learning, *Nurse Education Today*, 15 (2): 111–16.

Payne, M. (2000) *Anti-bureaucratic Social Work*. Birmingham: Venture Press.

Pennebaker, J. (1980) Self-perception of emotion and internal sensation, in D. Wenger and R. Vallacher (eds.) *The Self in Social Psychology*. New York: Oxford University Press.

Perron, B., Taylor, H., Glass, J. and Margerum-Leys, J. (2010) Information and communication technologies in social work, *Advances in Social Work*, 11 (2): 67–81.

Peters, T.J. and Waterman, R.H., Jr. (1982) *In Search of Excellence*. New York: Harper & Row.

Phung, T. (2014) Relationship based social work, in J. Lishman, C. Yuill, J. Brannan and A. Gibson (eds.) *Social Work: An introduction*. London: Sage.

Pizarro, D. (2000) Nothing more than feelings? The role of emotions in moral judgment, *Journal for the Theory of Social Behaviour*, 30 (4): 355–75.

Pooler, D., Wolfer, T. and Freeman, M. (2014) Finding joy in social work, II: Intrapersonal sources. *Social Work*, 59 (3): 213–21.

Quinney, A. (2006) *Collaborative Social Work Practice*. Exeter: Learning Matters.

Reamer, F. (2006) *Ethical Standards in Social Work: A review of the NASW code of ethics* (2nd edn.). Washington, DC: NASW Press.

Rogers, C. (1980) *A Way of Being*. Boston, MA: Houghton-Mifflin.

Roose, R., Mottart, A., Dejonckheere, N., Van Nijnattern, C. and De Bie, M. (2009) Participatory social work and report writing, *Child and Family Social Work*, 14 (3): 322–30.

Rosenberg, M. (1990) Reflexivity and emotions, *Social Psychology Quarterly*, 53 (1): 3–12.

Ruch, G. (2009) Identifying 'the critical' in a relationship based model of reflection, *European Journal of Social Work*, 12 (3): 349–62.

Ruch, G. (2012) Where have all the feelings gone? Developing reflective relationship-based management in child-care social work, *British Journal of Social Work*, 42 (7): 1315–32.

Ruch, G., Turney, D. and Ward, A. (eds.) (2010) *Relationship-based Social Work: Getting to the heart of practice*. London: Jessica Kingsley.

Rustin, M. (2005) Conceptual analysis of critical moments in Victoria Climbié's life, *Child and Family Social Work*, 10 (1): 11–19.

Saarni, C. (2000) Emotional competence: a developmental perspective, in R. Bar-On and J. Parker (eds.) *The Handbook of Emotional Intelligence*. San Francisco, CA: Jossey-Bass.

Salovey, P. and Mayer, J. (1989–90) Emotional intelligence, *Imagination, Cognition and Personality*, 9 (3): 185–211.

Schachter, S. and Singer, J. (1962) Cognitive, social and physiological determinants of emotional state, *Psychological Review*, 69 (5): 379–99.

Schön, D. (1983) *The Reflective Practitioner: How professionals think in action*. New York: Basic Books.

Scottish Government (2006) *Changing Lives: Report of the 21st century social work review*. Edinburgh: Scottish Government.

Scottish Social Services Council (SSSC) (2003) *The Framework for Social Work Education in Scotland*. Edinburgh: The Stationery Office.

Scottish Social Services Council (SSSC) (2004) *Codes of Practice for Social Service Workers and Employers*. Dundee: SSSC.

Scottish Social Services Council (SSSC) (2008) *The Framework for Continuous Learning in Social Services*. Dundee: SSSC/IRISS.

Scottish Social Services Council (SSSC) (2009) *Codes of Practice for Social Service Workers and Employers*. Dundee: SSSC.

Scottish Social Services Council (SSSC) (2011) *Social Media: Guidance and information for social service workers*. Dundee: SSSC.

Searle, J. (2010) *The Construction of Social Reality*. New York: Free Press.

Seden, J. (2011) The use of self and relationship: swimming against the tide, in J. Seden, S. Matthews, M. McCormick and A. Morgan (eds.) *Professional Development in Social Work: Complex issues in practice*. London: Routledge.

Senge, P. (1990) *The Fifth Discipline*. New York: Currency.

Senior, B. and Loades, E. (2008) Best practice as skilled organisational work, in K. Jones, B. Cooper and H. Ferguson (eds.) *Best Practice in Social Work: Critical perspectives*. Basingstoke: Palgrave Macmillan.

Sevenhuijsen, S. (1998) *Citizenship and the Ethics of Care: Feminist considerations on justice, morality and politics*. London: Routledge.

Slay, H. and Smith, D. (2011) Professional identity construction: using narrative to understand the negotiation of professional and stigmatized cultural identities, *Human Relations*, 64 (1): 85–107.

Smith, M. (2000) Supervision of fear in social work: a re-evaluation of reassurance, *Journal of Social Work Practice*, 14 (1): 17–26.

Social Care Institute for Excellence (SCIE) (2004) *Learning Organisations: A self-assessment resource pack*. London: SCIE.

Stanford, S. (2010) 'Speaking back to fear': responding to moral dilemmas of risk in social work practice, *British Journal of Social Work*, 40 (4): 1065–80.

Strongman, K. (1987) *The Psychology of Emotion*. Chichester: Wiley.

Taylor, B. (2010) *Reflective Practice for Healthcare Professional*. Maidenhead: Open University Press.

Taylor, B. (2011) *Working with Aggression and Resistance in Social Work*. Exeter: Learning Matters.

Taylor, C. (2003) Narrating practice: reflective accounts and the textual construction of reality, *Journal of Advanced Nursing*, 42 (3): 244–51.

Taylor, C. (2008) Trafficking in facts: writing practices in social work, *Qualitative Social Work*, 7 (1): 25–42.

Thomas, J. and Spreadbury, K. (2008) Making the best use of opportunities for supervision, learning and development to promote critical best practice, in H. Ferguson, K. Jones and B. Cooper (eds.) *Best Practice in Social Work: Critical perspectives*. Basingstoke: Palgrave Macmillan.

Thompson, N. (1998) *Promoting Equality: Challenging discrimination and oppression in the human services*. London: Sage.

Thompson, N. (2002) *People Skills*. London: Palgrave Macmillan.

Thompson, N. (2003) *Communication and Language: A handbook of theory and practice*. Basingstoke: Palgrave Macmillan.

Trevithick, P. (2003) Effective relationship-based practice: a theoretical explanation, *Journal of Social Work Practice*, 17 (2): 163–76.

Trevithick, P. (2005) *Social Work Skills*. Maidenhead: Open University Press.

Trevithick, P. (2011) Understanding defences and defensive behaviour in social work, *Journal of Social Work Practice*, 25 (4): 389–412.

Tripp, D. (1993) *Critical Incidents in Teaching: Developing professional judgement*. London: Routledge.

Turner, J. and Stets, J. (2005) *The Sociology of Emotions*. New York: Cambridge University Press.

Van Pelt, M., Hutschemaekers, G., Sleegers, P. and Hattum, N. (2015) Education for what? Exploring directions for the professionalisation of social workers, *British Journal of Social Work*, 45 (1): 278–95.

Walton, R. (2005) Social work as a social institution, *British Journal of Social Work*, 35 (5): 587–607.

Ward, A. (2010) The learning relationship: learning and development for relationship based practice, in G. Ruch, D. Turney and Ward (eds.) *Relationship-based Social Work: Getting to the heart of practice*. London: Jessica Kingsley.

Watling, S. and Rogers, J. (2012) *Social Work in a Digital Society*. London: Learning Matters.

Webb, S. (2001) Some considerations on the validity of evidence based practice in social work. *British Journal of Social Work*, 31 (1): 57–79.

White, S., Fook, J. and Gardner, F. (eds.) (2006) *Critical Reflection in Health and Social Care*. Maidenhead: Open University Press.

Whittaker, A. (2011) Social defences and organizational culture in a local authority child protection setting: challenges for the Munro Review?, *Journal of Social Work Practice*, 25 (4): 481–95.

Wiles, F. (2013) 'Not easily put into a box': constructing professional identity, *Social Work Education*, 32 (7): 854–66.

Wilson, K., Ruch, G., Lymbery, M. and Cooper, A. (2011) *Social Work: An introduction to contemporary practice*. London: Pearson.

Woodcock-Ross, J. (2011) *Specialist Communication Skills for Social Workers*. London: Palgrave Macmillan.

Yip, K. (2006) Self-reflection in reflective practice: a note of caution, *British Journal of Social Work*, 36 (5): 777–88.

Zapf, D. (2002) Emotion work and psychological wellbeing: a review of the literature and some conceptual considerations, *Human Resource Management Review*, 12 (2): 237–68.

Zirkel, S. (2000) Social intelligence: the development and maintenance of purposive behaviour, in R. Bar-On and J. Parker (eds.) *The Handbook of Emotional Intelligence*. San Francisco, CA: Jossey-Bass.

Index

Social Work, Poverty and Social Inclusion

Dave Backwith

ISBN: 978-0-335-24585-7 (Paperback)
eBook: 978-0-335-24586-4
2015

This book relates poverty and social exclusion to social work practice, offering a fresh approach to the challenges social workers face in helping clients out of poverty. *Social Work, Poverty and Social Inclusion* supports students in developing relationship-based and community-oriented approaches that can actively alleviate poverty.

Key features include:

- Numerous quotations and vignettes
- "What Do You Think?" exercises
- Explores the relation of poverty and social exclusion

www.openup.co.uk

OPEN UNIVERSITY PRESS

McGraw - Hill Education

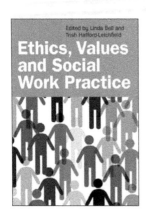

Ethics, Values and Social Work Practice

Linda Bell and Hafford-Letchfield

ISBN: 978-0-335-24529-I (Paperback)
eBook: 978-0-335-24530-7

2015

Ethics, Values and Social Work Practice is a brand new text offering students and social work practitioners a contemporary and relevant introduction to the central role of ethics and values in their work. This book offers a fresh perspective on ethics and values in the context of everyday social work practice, and provides an accessible route into the key theories, as well as useful strategies, tips and tools for practice.

Key features include:

- Discussion points for individual reflection or ethical debates
- Case studies based on likely scenarios from practice
- Chapter summaries and key points for social work practice

www.openup.co.uk

OPEN UNIVERSITY PRESS
McGraw - Hill Education